A MONSTROUS FEAST
A GUIDE TO FEEDING UNFAMILIAR GUESTS

By Phoebe Buskey

Original Illustrations by Atlit Pramudio

Copyright © 2025 by Phoebe Buskey
All Rights Reserved

ISBN 979-8-218-61935-0

Strange Moon Press LLC
10 Benning Street
Suite 160-168
West Lebanon, NH 03784-3404

www.strangemoonpress.com

A MONSTROUS FEAST
A GUIDE TO FEEDING UNFAMILIAR GUESTS

I was inspired to write this book while reading *The Bigfoot Files: The Reality of Bigfoot in North America* by David Hatcher Childress. There was a reference to reports of sasquatches searching for food in dumpsters and the speculation was that these individuals had been exiled or shunned by their families or clans, or who were too old to hunt.

It made me sad to think of an aging or displaced bigfoot scavenging for food on the outskirts of our communities—and so similar to the reality of many humans who are living and trying to survive on the margins of our society. I thought to myself, "If I saw a sasquatch scavenging for food, I would offer him a bowl of chili."

In many parts of the world, food is a valuable resource. Not everyone has access to fresh, healthy meals. Therefore, even if you don't share a common language, sharing food sends a very direct message: *I care about you, you are welcome here, and I want to share this precious resource with you.*

You'll probably never see a bigfoot rummaging through your trash. It's unlikely that you will encounter a chupacabra looking for a turkey dinner, and I doubt an insectoid alien will crash your next dinner party… but you might have a new neighbor who would appreciate a friendly welcome with a meal cooked in their honor. Maybe there's an individual in your community who doesn't have family with whom to share a holiday feast. Perhaps you know a busy single parent who would appreciate someone helping out with a meal for their family once or twice a month.

This guide will show you that you don't have to cook fancy, expensive foods to prepare a delicious, nourishing meal for the people you care about. Whoever you are cooking for, and for whatever reason, if you cook with love and compassion the results will always be delicious!

ATTENTION!

This book assumes that the reader has basic cooking skills. If you can fry an egg, cook pasta/rice, chop vegetables, and follow USDA guidelines for safe food handling and preparation, you can probably make any recipe in this book with a reasonable degree of success. Use common sense. All temperatures refer to the Fahrenheit scale. Don't make anything in this book if you're allergic to any of the ingredients. If you meet anything that seems challenging or encounter terms that you don't understand, please use your favorite internet search engine for more detailed instructions.

Table of Contents

The Big Guys — pg. 5

    Sasquatch (Chili) — pg. 6-7
    Yeti (Spicy Spinach & Tomato Daal) — pg. 8-9
    Skunk Ape Man (East Coast Steamed Clams, BBQ Sausage & Beans) — pg. 10-12
    Yowie (Rosemary & Garlic Lambchops) — pg. 13-14
    Batsquatch — pg. 15

Creatures from the Deep — pg. 17

    Gloucester Sea Serpent (Lobstah Rolls) — pg. 18-19
    Globsters (Seafood Surprise) — pg. 20-21
    Organism 46-B — pg. 22
    Kraken (Kraken® Spiced Rum Cake) — pg. 23-24
    Merfolk (Baked Lemony Salmon) — pg. 25-26

Visitors from Beyond the Stars — pg. 29

    Gray Aliens (Super Food Smoothie, Basic Quiche) — pg. 30-33
    Reptilians (Chef Salad) — pg. 33-34
    Nordics (Spinach Salad, Basic Vinaigrette) — pg. 35-36
    Insectoids (Turkey-Bacon Sliders with Chipotle Mayo) — pg. 37-38
    Hopkinsville Goblins — pg. 39

Freshwater Fiends — pg. 41

    Beast of Busco (Sugar Cream Pie) — pg. 42-43
    Champ (Pancakes with Vermont Maple Syrup and Bacon, Poutine) — pg. 44-46
    Lizardman of Scape Ore Swamp (Crawdads and Grits) — pg. 47-48
    Loveland Frogman — pg. 49
    Harry the Eel-Pig (Fried Fish and Hushpuppies) — pg. 50-51

The Wee Folk — pg. 53

    Gnomes (Mushroom Burgundy) — pg. 54-55
    Boggarts (Lancashire Hotpot) — pg. 56-57
    Duende (Basic Arepas) — pg. 58-59
    Menehune (SPAM® Fried Rice) — pg. 60-61
    Unicorns — pg. 62

Other Things That Go Bump in the Night — pg. 63

    Wampus Cat (Sausage Gravy and Biscuits) — pg. 64-65
    Chupacabra (Turkey Roll-Ups) — pg. 66-67
    Mothman (Strawberry Float, Ambrosia Salad) — pg. 68-69
    Snallygaster (Mamish Chicken and Gravy, Moravian Mints) — pg. 70-72

The Ultimate Beastly Feast — pg. 73

    Shrimp Cocktail Dip — pg. 75
    Roast Chicken — pg. 76
    Simple Mashed Potatoes — pg. 77
    Roast Parsnips and Carrots — pg. 78
    Summer Cake — pg. 79

SIGHTING/ENCOUNTER NOTES

THE BIG GUYS

**SASQUATCH
YETI
SKUNK APE MAN
YOWI**

SASQUATCH

Our main man, Sasquatch, is perhaps *the* quintessential American monster. Legends and myths of the tall, hairy, big-footed beast spread from the southernmost points of Florida to the northern coast of Maine and along the west coast to Alaska—not to mention everywhere in between! In fact, there been reported Bigfoot sightings in every state except Hawaii.

Of all the North American cryptids, there is perhaps more evidence of the existence of sasquatch than any other. In addition to countless eye-witness reports of sightings and encounters, cryptozoologists and other researcher have amassed a comprehensive collection of footprint casts, hair samples, photographs, as well as audio and video recordings that prove that this creature is real.

Bigfoot may be an evolutionary relative of *Gigantopithecus blacki*, a bipedal ape-like beast that stood approximately 10 feet tall and weighed around 600 pounds. Although *Gigantopithecus* is supposedly extinct, it is not unbelievable that a similar species of bipedal humanoid could remain in small populations throughout the world.

The typical adult male sasquatch stands between 7 to 12 feet tall, with a robust stature, sometimes a domed– or conical-shaped head, hirsute body and, of course, enormous feet.

According to cryptozoologists, sasquatch's diet consists of a combination of raw meat, fish, berries, and nuts.

If we use the human metabolism as a general guide, a 7-foot tall sasquatch weighing five hundred pounds would need a minimum of 5,000 calories per day to maintain strength, so it's not surprising that many sasquatch sightings suggest that the creature is almost always searching for food.

Sasquatch probably hunt, but they are also opportunistic feeders, meaning they'll take a meal wherever they can find one. They have been known to be drawn to the aroma of roasting meat and there have even been reports of bigfoots searching for food in dumpsters!

When a hungry sasquatch shows up on your property, he might like a big, hot bowl of spicy, protein-rich chili. To make this a real meal, serve it with warm crusty bread or rolls.

CLASSIC CHILI

This warm, classic chili is satisfying and very nutritious. This recipe calls for one can of black beans and one can of pinto beans, but you can use any combination that you have on hand.

Serves 4 to 6

Ingredients

- 1 lb. lean ground beef (or turkey)
- 1 large yellow onion, diced
- 2 cans of diced tomatoes with chilies (such as Rotel®,) 14 oz.
- 1 can black beans and 1 can pinto beans, drained and rinsed
- 1 cup of water
- 3 tablespoons chili powder
- 1 teaspoon each: smoked paprika, onion powder, garlic powder, cumin,
- ½ teaspoon cayenne pepper (or to taste)

Directions

- In a large pot or dutch oven, cook ground beef over medium heat, stirring frequently and breaking up any clumps so the meat is evenly crumbled. Move meat to one side and add onion, cook until tender and then stir into the beef.
- Add tomatoes, beans, and water, stir to mix into the beef and onion. Sprinkle seasonings and spices evenly over the top and stir until all ingredients are thoroughly blended.
- Simmer on low for 20 to 30 minutes.

If desired, serve with an assortment of add-your-own toppings such shredded cheddar cheese, sour cream, and diced avocado. Serve with crusty bread or rolls to round out the meal.

Cooking with Canned Beans

Canned beans are economical, versatile, healthful, and have a long shelf-life, making them ideal for everyday cooking. Although nutritional values vary slightly from bean to bean, they are generally low fat but high in protein and dietary fiber.

When using canned beans, it's always a good idea to rinse them well before adding them to your recipe. Rinsing removes up to 41% of the added sodium, which is especially important for those on reduced-sodium diets. Simply empty them into a colander over a sink and rinse with clear, cold water for a couple of minutes, then shake gently to drain and remove excess water.

YETI

Around 1889, English explorer Major Laurence Waddell, Professor of Tibetan Culture and Professor of Chemistry, traveling in disguise (the man believed to be the inspiration for *Indiana Jones*) was the first European to document the discovery of yeti footprints while exploring northeast Sikkim (an Indian state bordered by Tibet, Nepal, Bhutan, and West Bengal.) His guide explained that the prints had been created by a large, ape-like creature known to inhabit the highest, most remote regions of the Himalayan mountains.

In 1921, Lieutenant-Colonel Charles Howard-Bury was leading the British Mount Everest reconnaissance expedition when he comes across a set of tracks that his Sherpa guides tell him must have been created by the "Wild Man of the Snows" or, in their language, *metoh-kangmi*. Howard-Bury believed that the tracks have been made by a large gray wolf but did admit that in some places they appear to be prints of a bare-footed man.

Long known to the Indigenous peoples of the region, the yeti is believed to be a glacial spirit who brings fortune to native huntsman but can be a vicious and even lethal threat to outsiders who venture too far afield in the remote and treacherous region.

Even the esteemed and respected biologist Sir David Attenborough admitted, "I believe the Abominable Snowman may be real…If you have walked the Himalayas there are these immense forests that go on for hundreds of square miles which could hold the Yeti…it is not impossible that it might exist…"

Food sources are scarce in the high, remote regions of the Himalayas. According to Tibetan lore, the Yeti may live on a relatively meager diet of moss, amphibians, pikas (a small mammal belonging to the rabbit family,) although it's hard to imagine scraping up enough moss and frog legs to sustain the body mass of an enormous, muscular creature living in the extreme environment of a high altitude and freezing temperatures. Unless you have a couple of pika to roast over an open fire, the appetite of a hungry yeti could probably be satisfied with a bowl of India's most iconic comfort food: fragrant, spicy, nutritious daal.

SPICY TOMATO AND SPINACH DAAL

Lentils are a good source of protein, economical, and easy to prepare. This comforting vegetarian dish is more of a stew than a soup and is usually served over steamed basmati rice.

Serves 4

- Ingredients
- 4 ½ cups vegetable broth
- 1 cup of red lentils
- 1 medium onion, diced
- 2 cloves garlic, minced
- 2 tablespoons olive oil (or ghee, if you have it)
- 2 tablespoons red curry paste
- 1 teaspoon ground cumin
- ½ teaspoon turmeric
- ½ teaspoon cayanne pepper (or to taste)
- ½ teaspoon cinnamon
- 4 cups fresh spinach, roughly chopped
- 1 can diced tomatoes, 14.5 oz., any variety
- ¼ cup fresh cilantro, chopped

Directions

- Bring vegetable broth to a boil in a large soup pot or dutch oven. Add lentils, plus a pinch of salt if desired. Reduce heat to low. If a foam forms, skim it off. Simmer lentil over low heat for approximately an hour until lentils are tender.
- Meanwhile, heat oil on low in a small skillet or saucepan. Sauté garlic and onion until soft and slightly browned.
- Add spices (curry paste, cumin, turmeric, cayenne, and cinnamon.) Stir into garlic and onion, cook just a minute or two longer to let the spices warm. Add spinach, tomatoes, and cilantro. Continue to cook, stirring occasionally, until the spinach is wilted, about five minutes. Cover and set aside until the lentils are done.
- Add vegetable mixture to lentils and cook another 15 to 20 minutes. If desired, served over hot, steamed rice and with naan on the side.

The Himalayas

The crescent-shaped Himalayan Mountain range extends through five countries: Bhutan, China, India, Nepal, and Pakistan. All of these countries are rich in history, culture, and have distinct characteristics. Nepal is the most remote and isolated, so it's not surprising that many cryptozoologists believe this would be the most likely refuge of the reclusive yeti. The United Nations has officially recognized the "cultural significance" of the yeti in Nepali folklore, and the yeti is Nepal's national symbol.

SKUNK APE MAN

An inhabitant of swamps and marshes, a skunk ape can be considered Bigfoot's stinky southeastern cousin, the Sasquatch of the South. Like all our Big Guys, a skunk ape is a bipedal, ape-like creature. On average, a skunk ape is slightly shorter than a sasquatch, standing 5 to 7 feet tall, with reddish hair and a distinctly foul odor.

Skunk ape sightings have been reported in Florida, Georgia, and Alabama as early as 1818 although indigenous peoples knew of, and often interacted with, these "men" long before European settlers came along to record their presence.

There are a couple of theories surrounding the skunk ape's signature scent. The University of Florida's "Skunk Ape Research" project, led by Dr. Stanley Franklin, theorizes that the distinctive smell—described as a combination of skunk, rotten eggs, and dead fish—could be the result of the creature sheltering in abandoned alligator caves which contain high levels of methane.

Alternatively, skunk apes could have scent glands that emit the unpleasant, musky odor. Other primates such as gibbons, lemurs, and orangutans have scent glands that emit odor as a form of communication to others of their species, relaying information such as gender, social status, sexual readiness, and territorial boundaries.

A wild man was captured in 1884 near Ocheesee Pond in Jackson County, Florida. He was covered in hair and quite emaciated. It was reported at the time that he lived on a diet of berries and other foraged vegetation, although that seems to have been only speculation based on his weakened physical state.

Despite his hirsute appearance, his captors suspected that he was a mental asylum escapee, leading to the conclusion that he must have shown some spark of humanity or a certain degree of humanity. The wild man's captors enquired at nearby asylums and hospitals, but none of them admitted to have missing inmates. The captive was then taken by train to Tallahassee where his story—for us—comes to an end. His fate is unknown.

Since 2010, forty-eight of Florida's sixty-seven counties have documented reports of skunk ape sightings and there continue to be credible sightings throughout Georgia and Alabama.

Living in the deepest cypress swamps and marshes of the eastern South, one might think that skunk ape would take advantage of the rich diversity in his environment and feast on native crabs, clams, snails, but anecdotal evidence suggests that he is primarily an herbivore. This makes it a little harder to decide what he might like for dinner. Although it's what he is accustomed to, a handful of Florida swamp blueberries hardly seems generous and welcoming. Why not presume that he did break into a few clams occasionally and treat him to a plate full of steamers with melted butter? And if he looks really hungry, like the Ocheesee Wild Man, raid your pantry to whip up a big batch of BBQ Sausage and Beans to ensure he gets a hot, hearty meal that will nourish his body and soul.

EAST COAST STEAMED CLAMS

East Coast steamed soft-shells clams, sometimes simply called "steamers," are easy to prepare but may be an acquired taste for many. There are a lot of fancy recipes out there that include techniques such as steaming clams in white wine or sherry, adding seasonings like parsley and garlic, etc. but Skunk Ape Man probably likes to keep things simple. All you'll need for this recipe is clams, water, salt, melted butter, and (optional) fresh lemon wedges.

As a main dish, plan on about a pound of steamers per person. Remember, the bulk of the weight will be the shell, so this isn't as much as it seems! If you are serving steamers as an appetizer, plan for 4 to 6 clams per person.

For best flavor, start with the freshest clams you can get, but if you can't get them fresh off the boat you can still get great quality from a specialty seafood market or even the fish counter at your local grocery store. If possible, make your purchase on the same day you plan to serve them, but you can store them on ice in your fridge for an extra day if you need to. Select clams that are closed, without cracked shells.

Clean the clams by placing them in a bowl of cold water for ten to fifteen minutes. Some resources may suggest that you add a tablespoon of cornstarch but this isn't strictly necessary. Rinse the clams again, and if you want to take the time you can give them a little scrubbing with a soft vegetable brush to get off any remaining clinging sand or other debris.

As a main dish, plan on about a pound of steamers per person. Remember, the bulk of the weight will be the shell, so this isn't as much as it seems!

Fill a stock pot or deep sauce pan about 1/4 full with water and bring to a boil. Add one teaspoon of salt, then add the clams. You can use a steam rack if you want to, but it's fine to put the clams directly in the water. Cover the pot and remove from heat. Let sit for approximately 10 minutes while the steam does it's work. Take a peek—if the clams are open, they are ready! If you have used a steam rack, carefully lift it out, or if you have you can just carefully pour the clams and water out into a colander over the sink. Shake carefully to get any excess water out of the clams.

For added flavor, you can squeeze fresh lemon juice over the open clams before serving.

You'll see a little brown "leg" sticking out the side of the clam. Don't eat it! This is the clam's foot. You can use it as a handle to pull the clam out of its shell, then give the clam a swirl in melted butter. Bite the "belly" of the clam off of the foot, then discard both foot and shell.

BBQ SAUSAGE AND BEANS

The best thing about this easy stew is that it's endlessly adaptable to make use of nearly anything you have on hand. Start with a kielbasa or any other smoked sausage, add a couple of cans of beans and a bottle of your favorite barbeque sauce and you're good to go! Throw in some extra ingredients to get an even better, more nutritious meal that is sure to satisfy your hungriest guests.

Serves 6 to 8

Ingredients

- One smoked sausage, any variety such as…
    - Kielbasa
    - Chirozo
    - Andouille
- Two 14.5 oz cans of beans, drained and rinsed, any variety
    - Small red bean
    - Pinto
    - Kidney
    - Black
- One bottle (approx.. 16 oz.) prepared barbeque sauce, any variety
- 1 or 2 tablespoons vegetable oil
- Optional add-ins for extra nutrition and flavor
    - Diced onion
    - Diced red or green peppers
    - 14 oz. can diced tomatoes, any variety
- Hot, cooked rice (prepared according to package directions)

Directions

- Chop sausage into bite-sized pieces or slices
- Chop onion and peppers (optional)
- Drain/rinse beans.
- Heat oil in a large skillet (cast iron if possible)
- Add sausage, as well as onion and/or peppers if you're including them. Cook until vegetables are tender. Let the sausage get some browned, crispy bits to create a richer flavor.
- Add beans, and if you're using tomatoes you should add them now as well.
- Pour in the barbeque sauce and stir to blend. Set to simmer on low heat for 10 to 15 minutes, stirring occasionally. This gives the flavors a chance to blend.
- That's it! Serve over hot, cooked rice.

YOWIE

Lurking in the Australian outback, the yowie—a.k.a. yahweh, noocoonah, wawee, pangkarlangu, jimbra, just to name a few—is described as a creature who is nearly the same height as a human with extraordinarily long arms and, sometimes, feet that are "turned backwards."

Like all of the other big guys in this book, the yowie is a bipedal primate with human-like intelligence, a primal appetite, and an abundance of hair.

An elderly Aboriginal who went by the name of Old Bungaree told early settlers that there had once been tribes of yowie who were the original inhabitants of the country and referred to them as "an old race."

The earliest recorded sighting of a yowie by a European dates to 1789 and describes a wonderful beast that was nine feet tall. The yowie was reportedly captured in Botany Bay while it was sleeping and eventually taken to England where it was put on display. The fate of this creature is unknown, and some researchers believe the entire story was a hoax.

Like the American sasquatch, yowie are believed to build rudimentary structures with sticks and communicate by knocking branches against trees.

Another commonality is that some yowie and sasquatch are described as having talon-like fingers, but there is speculation that these are perhaps just very old individuals who have long, thickened, overgrown fingernails.

In the 1850s there were reports of indigenous apes or "hairy men of the woods" who harassed workers who were building a railroad, presumably in an attempt to stop the project. Several of the workers fought the yowie, who eventually gave up and progress on the railroad continued.

The yowie diets are similar to that of their distant American brethren, eating primarily wild game and fruits, nuts, and legumes. It is not unreasonable to think they have developed a taste for some of that world-famous Australian lamb. If you ever have the privilege of having a yowie at your dinner table, he would definitely be impressed if you served him a plate of juicy, succulent lamb chops.

ROSEMARY AND GARLIC LAMB CHOPS

Although maybe a little more expensive than beef, lamb is richer in omega-3 fatty acids and is generally considered to be a lean meat. It's also a good source of protein, iron, zinc, and vitamin B12. Lamb is easy cook and has a rich, strong flavor. This very simple recipe calls for shoulder chops.

Ingredients

- Lamb shoulder chops – one per guest
- Olive oil
- 3 sprigs fresh rosemary (or about 1 tablespoon dried)
- 1 clove fresh garlic, peeled and finely diced
- Coarsely ground sea salt and pepper

Directions

- Lightly salt and pepper chops on both sides.
- Preheat a large skillet (cast iron if possible) on low to medium heat.
- Gently sauté garlic until light brown.
- Increase heat to high and add chops and rosemary sprigs.
- Cook the chops for approximately 5 to 7 minutes on each side until browned and the internal temperature is 160° for medium or 170° for well-done.
- Lamb chops pair excellently with a simple side such as boiled or roast potatoes and any vegetable like asparagus, green beans, or fresh green peas.

DROP BEAR: The Other Australian Cryptid

The drop bear (scientific name *Thylarctos plummetus*) is a predatory koala-type creature that hangs around in trees and drops down on unsuspecting victims, often latching onto the neck with razor-sharp incisors… or so tourists are told.

Much like the American jackalope, the drop bear is an urban legend that locals love to pass off as a genuine threat.

In 2013, an April Fool's edition of the Australian Geographic ran a story claiming that tourists were more likely to be attacked by drop bears than the native population.

Whether there are drop bears living in Australia today or not, there is a factual basis for such a creature to exist. The Thylacoleo was "hypercarnivorous" marsupial that lived during the Late Pleistocene era that were believed to have weighed up over 200 lbs. and was an apex predator in Australia's ecosystem.

BATSQUATCH

This combination cryptid—as its name suggests—is half bat and half sasquatch. First sighted in the 1980s near Mt. Saint Helens, the creature resembles a flying primate in the tradition of the Jersey Devil, Mothman, and Southeast Asia's Orange Bati.

The appearance of Batsquatch is linked to the eruption of Mt. St. Helens, although the connection is not fully understood.

Could the eruption have opened a subterrain cavern in which the creature had been trapped for eons?

Witnesses describe the beast as being between nine and fifteen feet tall, having leathery wings, glowing eyes, a head like a wolf or bat, and a furry body.

Batsquatch has been sighted in Washington, California, and Ohio, and are thought to live in forested, mountainous regions.

Unfortunately, there are no clues in any of the sightings that might suggest what this beast likes to eat.

If Batsquatch shows up at your dinner party, you'll have to "wing it!"

COOKING NOTES

CREATURES FROM THE DEEP

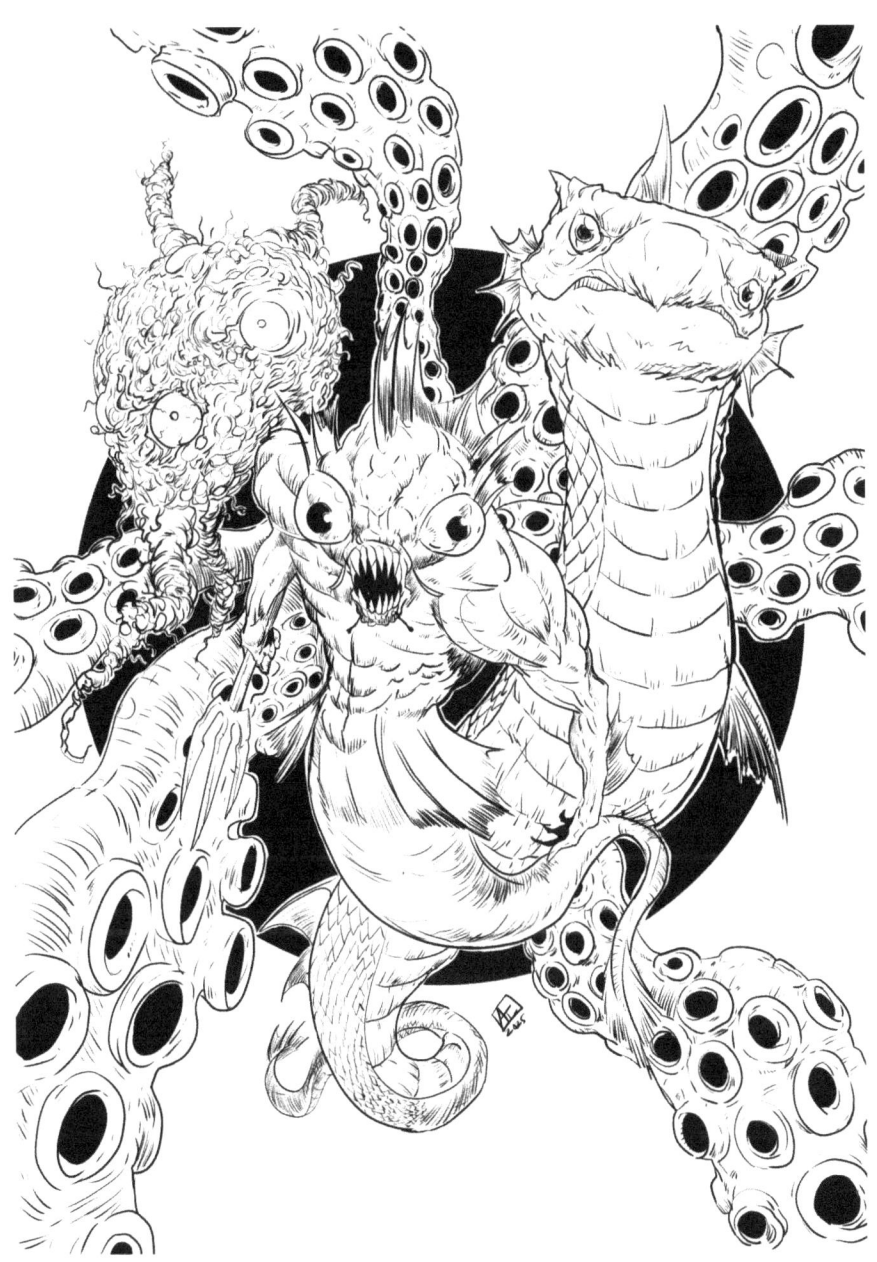

**GLOUCESTER SEA SERPENT
GLOBSTERS
KRAKEN
MERFOLK**

THE GLOUCESTER SEA SERPENT

The charming town of Gloucester, Massachusetts is picturesque coastal America at its best. Dotted with charming cottages, a busy fishing industry, and even a medieval-style castle, Gloucester is a delightful place to visit for those who love history, culture, shopping, and dining. Its waters are even home to a fearsome sea creature unimaginatively known simply as the Gloucester Sea Serpent. Sorry, it doesn't have a cute nickname like Nessie or Champ.

The first known recorded sighting of the Gloucester Sea Serpent was in 1817 (although it should be noted that the indigenous peoples of the region did warn settles of the creature much earlier) when a group of fishermen saw a serpentine beast with a head like a turtle swimming in the waters off the coast. Sometimes reported to have a humped-back body but often described as snake-like, there have been hundreds—if not thousands—of reported sightings throughout the years.

One interesting note is that almost all witnesses agree that the creature does not move in a side-to-side motion like a snake, but in an up-and-down or vertical motion.

Speculation that the Gloucester Sea Serpent is simply a "known but misidentified" marine animal does not hold up to scrutiny as many of the reported sightings come from experienced fishermen and mariners who *know* what local sea life looks like. If they say they are seeing something unusual, we should believe them! To date, this is one of the most well-documented sea serpents of all time.

When the Gloucester Sea Serpent slithers his way to your door for dinner, use your best Massachusetts accent to invite him in for a Gloucester Lobstah Roll.

Hammond Castle, Gloucester MA

The building of Hammond Castle began in 1926 and was completed in 1929 to be a home and laboratory for the inventor John Hays Hammond, Jr.

Hammond was known as the "Father of Remote Control" and held over 400 patents. He was an ardent collector who held medieval, Renaissance, and Roman artifacts and the building itself is constructed from architectural elements dating from the 15th, 16th, and 18th centuries. Hammond Castle is believed to be haunted by Mr. Hammond, who passed away in 1965. Witnesses to the hauntings have seen apparitions, and eerie images have been captured on film.

If you have the good fortune to tour Hammond Castle (now open to the public as a museum) keep an eye on the harbor—you may spot the Gloucester Sea Serpent swimming by!

LOBSTAH ROLLS

Lobster: You can do it the hard way or the easy way.

You can buy fresh New England (Atlantic) lobster at your local grocery store or fish market, steam it, crack the shells, and pick out the meat. It's a lot of work. Depending on where you live, you can expect to pay $12 to $18 per pound. Also keep in mind that when you buy a whole lobster by the pound, 70% is shell and only 30% is meat.

Alternatively, the seafood department may have canned, refrigerated lobster meat for $25 to $30 per pound. Expensive, yes, but it's going to be all meat, no shell, and *much* less work.

There are two varieties of lobster rolls—"hot buttered" or "lobster salad." Both delicious recipes are included here so you can give the Gloucester Sea Serpent his choice.

Lobstah rolls are traditionally served with a side of French fries, a cup of coleslaw, and a pint or two of cold beer.

Serves 3

Ingredients for Hot Buttered Lobstah Rolls

- 1 lb. North Atlantic lobster meat
- 2 to 4 tablespoons hot, melted butter
- 1 lemon, quartered
- 3 large hot dog buns or sub rolls, lightly toasted

Directions

- Divide lobster between the toasted buns/rolls.
- Squeeze a wedge of fresh lemon over the lobster, then follow with a drizzle of hot, melted butter, approximately 1 or 2 tablespoons per roll (go with your instinct.)
- Serve fresh.

Ingredients for Lobstah Salad Rolls

- 1 lb. North Atlantic lobster meat
- ½ cup mayonnaise
- ¼ cup finely diced celery
- 1 tablespoon fresh lemon juice
- 2 teaspoons fresh finely chopped dill (optional)
- 3 large hot dog buns or sub rolls, lightly toasted

Directions

- In a large bowl, mix all ingredients. Chill for 20 minutes to one hour.
- Divide between buns/rolls.
- Serve fresh

GLOBSTERS

Globsters aren't a specific cryptid in the same way that most of those featured in this book are. The term "globster" was coined by Ivan T. Sanderson in 1962 and is defined as an unidentifiable organic creature or mass that washes up on the shoreline on an ocean.

Not all globsters are the same. Some have tentacles but cannot be positively identified as a known cephalopod. Some have long necks and heavy bodies, like a plesiosaur or other prehistoric beast believed to be long extinct. There have been multiple creatures dubbed globster throughout the years and although some of them have supposedly been identified though DNA testing, a significant number remain unknown.

Globsters remind us that there are still enormous, unidentified beasts living in the oceans of the world.

Also, it's really fun to say the word *globster*.

In 1924 a creature that would now be described as a globster washed up on Margate Beach in South Africa.

This story is a bit unusual because it is perhaps the only one in which the cryptid in question was seen alive—and battling two killer whales—before its carcass washed ashore days later.

The beast was dubbed "Trunko" and was described as having an elephant-like trunk and covered in white fur somewhat like a polar bear.

In 2017, after studying rediscovered photos of Trunko, paleontologist Dr. Darren Naish stated, "The idea that this was really the body of a white-furred, trunked sea monster stems from naivety about the appearance of rotting animal carcasses," and goes on to attribute the white fur of the creature to "the large amount of what looks like frayed, badly decayed collagen…"

However, Dr. Naish's dismissive explanation does not account for the fact that the farmer who saw Trunko fighting the two killer whales *also* described the beast as having white fur. It's hard to imagine how a creature with frayed, badly decaying collagen would be able to fight anything.

Since globsters are the remains of several different unidentified species, speculating on their dietary preferences is a challenge. Fish, eels, shellfish, plankton, kelp… virtually anything living in the vast oceans could be fair game. If you're lucky enough to encounter a live globster, celebrate the occasion and offer it a dish that contains a variety of seafood, such as Seafood Surprise.

SEAFOOD SURPRISE

Three kinds of seafood are baked in a rich sauce of cream and sherry, served on hot cooked pasta such as spaghetti, farfalle, or cavatappi, and topped with freshly shaved parmesan cheese. This recipe is a decadent indulgence that is perfect for special occasions.

Seafood Surprise pairs well with a side salad and white wine.

Serves 5

Ingredients

- 1 lb. sea scallops
- 1 lb. large shrimp, peeled and deveined, tails removed
- 1 lb. cod and/or haddock loin, cut into cubes approximately 1" square
- 2 large shallots, peeled and finely sliced
- 1 clove garlic, peeled and finely minced
- 1 teaspoon Old Bay Seasoning
- 1 ½ cups heavy cream
- 1 tablespoon cooking sherry
- 1 tablespoon lemon juice
- Olive oil
- 3 tablespoons salted butter
- ½ cup Italian style dry breadcrumbs
- 1 lb. spaghetti or linguine, cooked according to package directions
- Freshly shaved parmesan cheese, for garnish

Directions

- Preheat oven to 375 degrees.
- Lightly grease a small casserole dish or deep pie plate.
- Place the scallops, shrimp, and fish in the dish, alternating types of seafood so each serving will get an equal amount of each kind. Set aside.
- In a small saucepan, sauté shallots and garlic until tender and fragrant. Slowly whisk in cream, sherry, lemon juice, and Old Bay Seasoning. Cook over very low heat, stirring occasionally, until the mixture begins to thicken slightly.
- Carefully pour the cream mixture over the seafood.
- Melt the butter in a bowl or glass measuring cup and stir in the breadcrumbs until all the butter is absorbed. Sprinkle lightly over the top of the casserole.
- Baked in preheated oven for 25 to 35 minutes, or until all seafood is cooked through and topping is golden brown.
- Serve over hot cooked pasta, generously top with shaved parmesan.

Organism 46-B

The creature known as Organism 46-B was supposedly found in a subterranean, subglacial lake beneath two miles of ice near Vostock Station, a Russian research facility located in Antarctica.

Details of the phenomenal discovery are as murky as the waters the beast was found in, but some tantalizing details did bubble to the surface.

The organism is rumored to be a prehistoric cephalopod approximately 33 feet long and displayed a high degree of intelligence. Additionally, the creature was able to shape-shift and can telepathically control other animals.

According to many cryptid and conspiracy blogs, Organism 46-B killed several Russian scientists in a variety of gruesome ways before it was eventually captured.

Predictably, the Russian government silenced the remaining members of the team and now officially deny the discovery altogether.

If you hear the voice of Organism 46-B telepathically summoning you to bring him a snack, make a good tin-foil hat and remind yourself that this creature is *probably* just an urban legend.

KRAKEN

The legend of the fearsome kraken dates back to approximately 1180, when King Sverre of Norway wrote of a beast in the waters surrounding Iceland, Greenland, and Norway. The word kraken is believed to be a derivative of the Old Norse word *krake*, which meant something twisted or curled, likely a reference to the monster's many reaching, grasping tentacles.

In 1746, the Swedish naturalist Carl Linnaeus acknowledged the kraken as a real animal and classified it as a type of cuttlefish in his book, *Fauna Svecica*. Today, mainstream scientists believe that ancient reports of the kraken were actually sightings of the giant squid, which can easily grow to 50 feet in length.

The kraken, however, was described as beast that was much, much larger. The creature of lore was so large that it was sometimes mistaken for a landmass. With tentacles the size of masts, a kraken could easily take down a ship and devour the entire crew.

In January of 2023, an underwater camera in the Antarctic Ocean (also known as the Southern Ocean) captured video of a colossal squid. Although not as long as giant squid, colossal squid are larger in mass and have swiveling hooks on their tentacles that aid in the capture of prey.

Could the kraken really be a colossal squid rather than a giant squid, or something altogether yet unknown to science?

If a monstrous giant or colossal squid is really lurking in the depths of the icy northern seas, he would certainly be partial to seafood. However, it's not just any legendary sea monster that gets a rum brand named after him! The Kraken would undoubtedly feel honored if you presented him with a delicious slice of decadent, buttery Kraken® Spiced Rum Cake.

THE TROLLS OF NORWAY

Trolls have been an integral part of Norwegian culture and folklore for thousands of years. Stories of trolls in Norse literature begin in the 1200s in sagas and poetic works such as the Poetic Edda and the Prose Edda.

Whether trolls are a threat to humans or not is a matter of debate. Early stories indicate that trolls are simply benign creatures, neither good nor evil, who are somewhat slow and perhaps dimwitted. Trolls range in size from gigantic to tiny. Some have only one eye, and some have multiple heads.

Legend states that trolls are nocturnal because the sun will turn them to stone. In fact, there are numerous troll-shaped rock formations throughout the country that are thought to be trolls who were turned to stone after having been touched by sunlight.

KRAKEN® SPICED RUM CAKE

This is a rich, moist, delicious twist on classic golden rum cake. For the best results, use a bundt pan. It's important to leave the cake in the pan while it cools to let the rum syrup really soak in.

Serves **8** to 10

Ingredients

- Spice cake mix, such as Betty Crocker Super Moist® (requires 1 cup water, 1/3 cup vegetable oil, and 3 eggs)
- ¾ cup butter
- ½ cup Kraken®, any variety
- ¼ cup water
- 1 cup brown sugar
- 3 cups confectioner's sugar
- 3 to 4 tablespoons water
- 1 teaspoon vanilla extract

Directions

- Bake cake in bundt pan according to package directions.
- On low heat, melt butter in a small saucepan. Add brown sugar and stir to blend. Add water and rum, continue stirring until all ingredients are thoroughly homogenized. Continue stirring and cooking on low heat until a slightly thickened syrup has formed.
- Slowly—very slowly—pour hot rum syrup evenly over the cake, allowing it to soak into the cake.
- Let the cake sit, still in the pan, as you prepare the glaze: In a large bowl, combine confectioner's sugar and vanilla extract. Add 2 tablespoons of water and stir, continue adding water by ½ tablespoons until it's just thin enough to drizzle.
- Turn the cake out onto a plate. If you think it's going to stick, you can gently slide a rubber spatula down the sides and around the center to loosen it up. Drizzle the glaze over the cake in a zig-zag motion.
- Cut into **8** to 10 slices to serve.

MERFOLK

Stories of merfolk date back to the very earliest known written language. The Sumerian texts, known as "The Epic of Gilgamesh," written around 2000 B.C., refers to fish-women, and the Sumerian religion includes a tale of a heroic mermaid called Kuli-ana who was slain by a god named Ninurta.

Around one thousand years later, another mermaid appears in the same region (modern day Iraq and Syria) as a goddess named Atargatis. Myths and stories of merfolk—both mermaids and mermen—persist throughout various cultures and across the globe from then on. Almost every ancient civilization in the world has merfolk mythology.

The merfolk mythos does not subside with the passing of time. Byzantine and Greek legends have several stories of merfolk, and these beguiling creatures feature prominently in the medieval literature of Norway, Germany, Sweden, and the British Isles.

Merfolk appear in Chinese, Korean, Japanese, and Indian folklore. Could the enduring stories surrounding merfolk be evidence that these entities really exist? It would be easy to dismiss the legends of mermaids as fanciful works of fiction, or to attribute the many sightings as the ignorance of our ancestors who just didn't understand what they were seeing in the waters around the world. However, there are many modern and present-day sightings of merfolk that cannot be explained away so easily.

In 1967, a ferry full of tourists near the Mayne Islands of British Columbia spotted a mermaid with long blonde hair sitting on the beach eating a salmon. The passengers got such a good look at her that one witness even claimed that the mermaid had dimples!

Luckily, this mermaid sighting tells us exactly what we need to know when hungry merfolk crash your dinner party. Salmon is not only delicious, but also a great source of protein, vitamin B6, and magnesium.

BAKED LEMONY SALMON

Get Atlantic salmon fillet for this recipe if you can, but any good fresh salmon will work. This is an easy but elegant dish that pairs well with a side of couscous or rice pilaf. You'll need a small baking or casserole dish that's long enough to accommodate the fillet.

Serves 4

Ingredients

- 1 lb. boneless salmon fillet or 4 pre-cut portions of 4 oz. each
- 2 lemons—one sliced, one cut into wedges
- 1 cup Castelvetrano pitted olives (or other mild green pitted olive)
- 1 ½ cups grape or cherry tomatoes
- ¼ cup fresh basil (optional)
- 1 tablespoon dried dill
- Olive oil
- Ground black pepper

Directions

- Preheat oven to 350 degrees.
- Slice one lemon into eight thin slices and arrange in two rows of four slices in the center of the baking sheet.
- Lay the fillet on top of the lemon slices, skin side down. The lemon here keeps the salmon slightly off the bottom of the dish and helps to impart flavor but not necessarily meant to be served along with the salmon.
- Brush the top of the fish with about a teaspoon of olive oil, then sprinkle with dill and black pepper.
- Arrange the olives, tomatoes, and basil in the dish evenly around the salmon.
- Drizzle a little more olive oil (approximately one or two tablespoons) over the tomatoes and olives.
- Cover tightly and bake for approximately 20 minutes, until nearly done.
- Uncover and continue baking until the top of the salmon is lightly brown and the fish easily flakes with a fork.
- Divide fish into four portions and serve warm, topping liberally with the olives and tomatoes. Serve with additional lemon wedges on the side.

You can grow fresh basil!

You don't need outdoor space or a green thumb to successfully grow basil. You can grow easily fresh basil on a sunny windowsill (or under a grow light.) It's well worth the minimal effort of upkeep.

You can start basil from seed, but most large grocery stores sell live basil plants in small pots in their produce department for just a few dollars. Each plant will provide you with a constant, fresh supply of basil leaves. Simply pick off the leaves you want to use and you'll see new growth forming in a matter of days. Trim back periodically to keep your basil plant compact, tidy, and productive.

TIPS FOR MEAL PLANNING

- When you're trying to decide what to make for dinner at the end of a busy day, you are more likely to prepare something that's quick, easy, and familiar, which leads to making the same things over and over. Take the time to create a weekly meal plan to reduce the risk of repetition. Base each meal around a primary protein such as poultry, legumes, fish/seafood, beef, pork, tofu, cheese, and eggs. This doesn't mean that the protein must be the main ingredient, but it's a good starting point to ensure variety throughout the week.

- To find new recipes and inspiration, check websites of your go-to grocery brands. Which do you reach for most often? Ore-Ida®, Pastene®, Goya®, Betty Crocker®, Jiffy®, Kikkoman®, and many others all have a treasure trove of great recipes on their sites. Subscribe to their email list to get even more recipes, new item notifications, coupons, and special offers.

- Many large grocery chains offer free, quarterly publications featuring new items, seasonal recipes, regional-interest stories, and sometimes a coupon or two. Usually, the recipes will include store-brand ingredients that are cheaper than their brand-name counterparts.

- Make note of family favorites. Which recipes are requested most often? Look for similar recipes with variations—or make up your own!—to keep favorites from getting boring. For example, if your family really loves lasagna, try 'em all: pepperoni lasagna, chicken taco lasagna, vegetable lasagna, etc.

SIGHTING/ENCOUNTER NOTES

VISTORS FROM BEYOND THE STARS

**GRAYS
REPTILIANS
NORDICS
INSECTOIDS**

GRAY ALIENS a.k.a "Zeta Reticulians"

Gray aliens, sometimes simply known as grays, are perhaps the most recognized alien species in modern popular culture. Believed to come from the Zeta Reticuli star system, these extraterrestrial biological entities are typically described as being short in stature with smooth gray skin and bulbous heads. They have large black eyes but very tiny noses and mouths.

Some people have reported that Grays bring a message of interplanetary peace, show concern for humanity's technological development, and an interest in preserving the environment. Yet others claim they have been abducted by Grays and were unwilling subjects of medical experimentation that included the implantation of alien technology and getting "probed."

Regardless of the motive for their visits, they are here, and they are probably hungry.

Given that Zeta Reticuli is approximately 39 lights years away, Grays traveling to and from our galaxy have probably developed a taste for nutrient-dense foods that are also easy to transport and have a long shelf life. Seeds, nuts, and legumes are obvious choices that fit these criteria, along with freeze-dried produce like kale, avocados, and berries that can endure a long journey through space. A superfood smoothie might be just the thing to satisfy the appetite of a traveler from beyond the stars!

But if you want to serve something that is a little more substantial—a real meal—the next thing to consider is the size of a Gray's mouth (very small, by most accounts) and how they consume their food. Nobody who has met an alien Gray reported that they flashed a mouthful of pearly whites, but it seems reasonable to assume they would have at least rudimentary teeth.

Still, we probably don't want to challenge our new friend's chewing capability by presenting them with a medium-rare T-bone steak! A Gray would probably prefer to tuck into an easy-to-eat, eco-friendly quiche made with free-range eggs and organic cheese.

What is a light year?

A light year is a measurement of distances between two objects in the vastness of outer space, defined as the length of time it takes for light to travel in one year.

Light travels at a rate of 5.88 million miles in one year.

The star system known as Zeta Reticuli is about 39.17 light years away from our solar system.

This means our Zeta Reticulian friends have traveled a little over two hundred, thirty million miles to get here.

Super Food Smoothie

This great energy-booster is quick and easy to make for a nutritious breakfast or satisfying snack.

Serves 1

Ingredients

- 1 ¼ cup almond milk (unflavored or vanilla)
- ½ cup unsweetened Greek yogurt
- 1 cup baby spinach or kale (thick stalks or stems removed)
- 1 tablespoon flaxseed meal
- 1 ½ cup frozen blueberries, strawberries, raspberries or mixed
- 1 tablespoon honey or other natural sweetener* (optional)

Directions

- Put all of the ingredients into a blender and blend until smooth.
- Thin with additional almond milk until desired consistency, if needed.
- Pour into glass and serve immediately.

*Please don't serve chemical or artificial sweeteners to our friends from outer space. Aspartame, specifically, has been classified by American Institute for Cancer Research (AICR) as a possible carcinogen. Ingesting this chemical is unnecessary and simply not worth the risk.

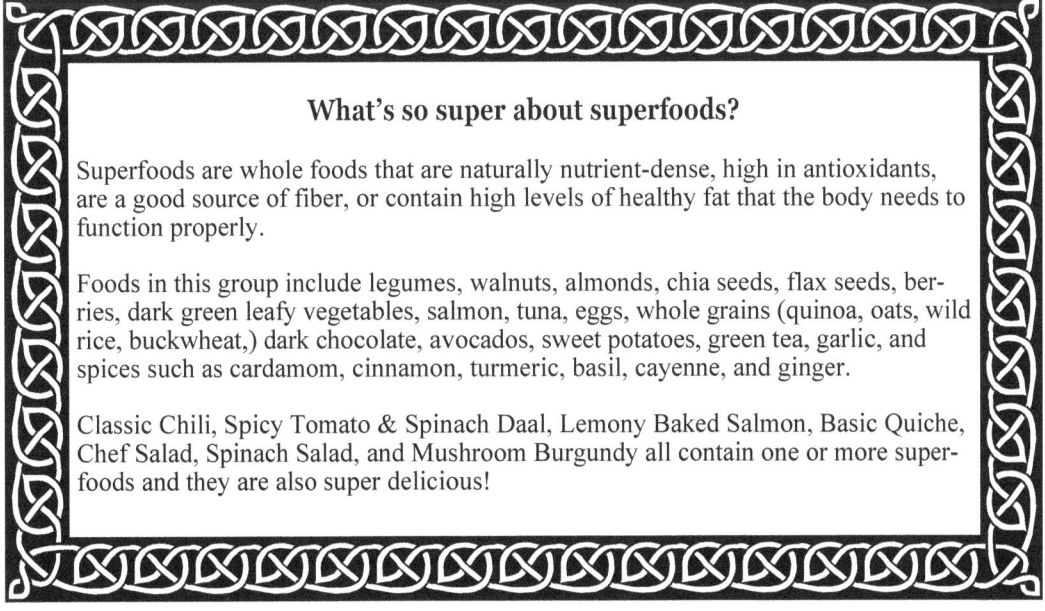

What's so super about superfoods?

Superfoods are whole foods that are naturally nutrient-dense, high in antioxidants, are a good source of fiber, or contain high levels of healthy fat that the body needs to function properly.

Foods in this group include legumes, walnuts, almonds, chia seeds, flax seeds, berries, dark green leafy vegetables, salmon, tuna, eggs, whole grains (quinoa, oats, wild rice, buckwheat,) dark chocolate, avocados, sweet potatoes, green tea, garlic, and spices such as cardamom, cinnamon, turmeric, basil, cayenne, and ginger.

Classic Chili, Spicy Tomato & Spinach Daal, Lemony Baked Salmon, Basic Quiche, Chef Salad, Spinach Salad, and Mushroom Burgundy all contain one or more superfoods and they are also super delicious!

BASIC QUICHE

The secret to making this quiche really stand out is to use the best possible quality ingredients available. Any chicken eggs will work perfectly fine but choose free-range chicken eggs if possible or duck eggs for more delectable results!

Serves 4 to 6

Ingredients

- 1 nine-inch pie crust
- 2 cups half-and-half
- 4 medium chicken eggs or 3 duck eggs
- ¼ teaspoon salt
- ¼ teaspoon white pepper
- ¼ teaspoon nutmeg
- 4 ounces shredded sharp cheddar
- 2 ounces shredded mozzarella cheese
- Smoked paprika (optional)

Directions

- Preheat oven to 425°
- In a large bowl, combine half-and-half, salt, and eggs, then beat well, until thoroughly blended. Stir in pepper, nutmeg, and cheese.
- Carefully pour into prepared pie shell. If desired, lightly sprinkle the top with smoked paprika.
- Bake for 15 minutes, then reduce heat to 350° and bake for another 15 to 20 minutes or until crust is golden brown and the filling is set (not jiggly or runny.) Remove from oven and allow to set undisturbed for another 5 to 10 minutes.
- Cut into wedges and serve warm.
- To make a complete meal, serve with Spinach Salad.

Dare to Use Duck Eggs

If you have never tried cooking or baking with duck eggs, the prospect of doing so may seem intimidating, but there's really nothing to worry about. Duck eggs have a lot of benefits. Duck eggs have thicker shells than chicken eggs, which means they don't spoil as quickly. They are also higher in protein, iron, and vitamins A, B6, B12, and E.

Available at many poultry farms, farmer's markets, or specialty co-ops, duck eggs are delicious, nutritious, and just as easy to cook as chicken eggs.

Duck eggs have a slightly different flavor than chicken eggs, so if you are eating them "straight up" (fried, poached, scrambled, etc.) you might notice, but the difference in flavor is unlikely to be detected in baking and this is where duck eggs really shine! The rich yolks add decadence to baked goods such as cakes, brownies, cookies, custards, and more.

REPTILIANS

Alien reptilians have been known in various forms throughout human history. Ancient Egyptian carvings and texts refer to "gods" such as the crocodile-headed Sobek and the snake-man Atum. India has stories of the nagas, a race of beings that were half snake and half man, and in ancient Rome the god called Glycon was believed to have the body of a snake and the head of a man. All these creatures are recorded as flesh-and-blood entities who directly interact with humanity. To be thought of as gods they must have had divine abilities, supernatural powers or, as many ancient alien theorists believe, highly advanced technology that made early humans view them in this way.

Humans who encounter reptilians today, usually in the context of abduction, rarely have good things to say about their experiences.

Unlike the Nordics who are believed to have an agenda of peace, or the more neutral insectoids, reptilians give off a decidedly sinister vibe. Even the gray aliens who are known to conduct nonconsensual medical experiments on their abductions victims don't seem as nefarious as the reptilians.

Some extreme conspiracy theorists believe that shape-shifting reptoids in human form have infiltrated the highest levels of governments worldwide and will soon reveal their true identities to become overlords of humanity.

However, if the reptilian agenda is to "divide and conquer" humanity, they have had around 5,000 years to accomplish their goal.

Hmm… seems like they aren't in any hurry.

Maybe the reptoids are just misunderstood and need a few good friends.

If you're even abducted by a reptilian (or if they come knocking on your front door like a respectable guest) offer them a drink and a bite to eat.

The diets of ordinary terrestrial reptiles vary from species to species: Komodo dragons are carnivorous apex predators, but green iguanas are herbivores. Other reptiles fall somewhere in between. So, what to feed a hungry reptilian that could be either a vegetarian or a carnivore?

A delicious chef salad loaded with a variety of fresh vegetables, ham, cheese, and turkey would be suitable for whatever they prefer and will definitely be a great way to demonstrate your hospitality.

CHEF SALAD

Full of fresh veggies that are rich in nutrients and filling enough to be a main course, chef salad makes a great lunch or a light evening meal. Use a mix of dark leafy greens such as spinach, arugula, and beet greens.

Serves 4

Ingredients

- Four to five cups mixed fresh greens, roughly torn or chopped into bite-sized pieces
- 6 radishes, thinly sliced
- ½ large red onion, thinly sliced into rounds and then cut in halves or quarters
- 3 small tomatoes, each cut into 6 to 8 wedges each
- 1 medium cucumber, peeled, sliced into rounds approx. 1/8" thick
- ½ lb. thinly sliced deli ham, any variety
- ½ lb. thinly sliced deli turkey, any variety
- 8 oz. Fresh mozzarella cheese "pearls" such as BelGioioso®
- Dressing, any variety, although French, creamy Italian, or Thousand Island all work particularly well with this salad
- Croutons (optional)

Directions

- Wash, chop/peel/slice/dice all vegetables accordingly.
- Place all vegetables in a large salad bowl and toss together.
- Divide vegetables amongst four large salad bowls, making sure each bowl gets approximately the same amount of each ingredient.
- On a cutting board or kitchen work surface, lay one slice of ham on top of one slice of turkey and roll them together (relatively tightly) and then slice the roll into rounds. Repeat with remaining slices.
- Dress the salads—approximately 2 tablespoons per bowl, or to taste.
- Divide all the sliced rolls of meat among the bowls of vegetables, making a nice arrangement around the top.
- Divide cheese pearls in the same manner and add croutons if desired.
- Serve while fresh.

NORDICS

Of all the alien species that are thought to be walking among us, none are considered more peaceful and benevolent than Nordics. Hailing from the Pleiades, and believed by some to be angels, the Nordics are an ancient alien race that may have been living on—or in—Earth since the beginning of human history.

In various cultures the Nordics are known as "True White Brothers," "Tall Whites," or "Space Brothers." With their golden or reddish-blonde hair and bright blue eyes, these statuesque aliens easily blend in with their human "brothers."

Although the Nordics have lived amongst us for millennia, it was not until the 1950s when George Adamski introduced their presence to popular culture. In his three books, *Flying Saucers Have Landed*, *Inside the Space Ships*, and *Flying Saucers Farewell*, he not only describes meeting with the Nordics but also traveling with them aboard their spaceships. Adamski's texts claim that the Nordics come from Venus and "other planets in Earth's solar system," but many ancient alien researchers believe that the Nordics reside in a secret inner earth realm called Agartha. Both beliefs could be true: Nordics may have originally been inhabitants of other planets but now reside within our Earth, or the citizens of Agartha may be only a small group of immigrants while primary populations dwell elsewhere.

The main issue with Agartha lies in the question of lighting. How could a an entire civilization live and thrive in the dark?

Hollow-Earth theorists have a couple of ideas about that. The first theory is that there may be phosphorescent life (such a plants and fungus) in enough abundance to provide adequate lighting for day-to-day tasks. Another theory, made popular in the 17th century by English astronomer and physicist Edmond Hailey, is that there is a "core" of energy floating in the center of the earth, something like a miniature sun.

The most likely scenario however (since we are talking about a race of highly advanced beings) is that they have developed technology to create artificial lighting that is sufficient for their needs.

If the Nordics have truly been living below the surface of the earth in the subterranean land of Agartha for eons, we may make some suppositions about their diet. We know that they are peaceful and compassionate. They are probably vegetarians, if not vegans. It's unlikely that they would be enthusiastic about chowing down on a huge rack of barbeque ribs or a big venison stew.

The Nordics would probably be more comfortable eating the kinds of foods that could be easily grown or harvested in the Earth's interior. The first obvious choice would be mushrooms, which are rich in nutrients. There are many vegetables that grow in low-light conditions such as root vegetables like carrots, parsnips, radishes, and beets, as well as leafy greens like lettuce and spinach. If they have domesticated any type of animal as a source of food, it would probably be for the harvesting of milk or eggs rather than for meat. Cheese is a great source of protein and would be easy for inner earth dwelling beings to produce. Therefore, we can confidently speculate that your Nordic alien dinner guests may enjoy a fresh, nutrient-rich simple green salad with delicious grilled halloumi cheese.

SPINACH SALAD

This is a quick and easy salad that makes a light main meal or a satisfying side dish. You'll need a skillet grill or indoor grill for the halloumi cheese.

Serves 4

Ingredients

- 4 cups baby spinach, torn or chopped to bite-size
- 1 red onion, finely sliced
- 2 cups white button mushrooms, chopped
- ½ cup radishes, finely sliced
- 1 block halloumi cheese, 8.8oz.
- Croutons (any variety)
- Olive oil
- Basic vinaigrette (recipe below)

Directions

- Brush grill with olive oil and cook the halloumi on medium heat. It will get nicely browned but won't melt! Flip once to get both sides done. Cut into bite-sized cubes.
- Coarsely chop spinach
- Toss spinach, onion, mushrooms, and radishes in a large salad bowl
- Top with cheese and croutons
- Divide evenly among four small salad bowls
- Serve with basic vinaigrette (tastes vary, so allow guests to dress their own bowls)

BASIC VINAIGRETTE

Easy, classic vinaigrette makes a great dressing that can be used for nearly any kind of green salad. The most basic version is simply a ratio of one part vinegar to three parts virgin olive oil. Seasonings are optional. This recipe calls for white wine vinegar, but feel free to experiment with other varieties.

Makes about one cup of dressing

Ingredients

- ¼ cup white wine vinegar
- ¾ cup virgin olive oil
- 1 teaspoon lemon juice

Directions

- Combine all ingredients in a bowl
- Whisk briskly until thoroughly combined
- Serve fresh, before vinegar and oil begin to separate

INSECTOIDS

Sometimes known as mantids or mantoids, the insectoids are believed by some alien researchers to have originated in the Draco solar system. As their name suggests, insectoids are somewhat mantis- or ant-like in appearance, featuring triangular heads, multifaceted eyes, and exoskeleton bodies.

According to eyewitness accounts, insectoids are roughly the same size as humans or slightly taller, which can be quite frightening for people who suffer from entomophobia, but in most cases of human/insectoid encounters the alien visitors have shown themselves to have a calm and peaceful nature. They have reportedly used holographic technology and telepathy to communicate with humans, displaying predictive warnings of the fate of the planet.

Abductees often report that insectoids are in the company of small, gray aliens, suggesting that they are working together. One abductee estimated that the mantoid she met was approximately seven feet tall.

We can probably assume that insectoids are as adaptable as their terrestrial cousins when it comes to their climate and environment, but what about their dietary needs? Let's take some clues from the food that Earth-bound insects enjoy.

Praying mantises are carnivores. They prey on other insects such as flies, moths, beetles, crickets, ants, etc., but it's unlikely that you are going to serve a plate full of bugs at your dinner party. Instead, provide your insectoid guests with the protein they crave by cooking up a batch of Turkey-Bacon Sliders with homemade chipotle mayo.

Arthropleura

Could there really be an species of insect that is as large, or larger, than a human?

The Arthropleura were a type of arthropod that lived approximately 290 million years ago.

These invertebrates were roughly 6 to 8.5 feet long with an appearance similar to the modern-day millipede. These creatures are believed to have lived in open environments and may have been amphibious. The Arthropleura was likely carnivorous and fed on small, soft-bodied creatures.

Although mainstream science believes Arthropleura to be extinct, it's possible that revenant specimens still exist in remote, undisturbed regions of the globe.

TURKEY-BACON SLIDERS WITH CHIPOTLE MAYO

These yummy turkey mini-burgers are served on slider rolls with sliced avocado, bacon, and homemade chipotle mayonnaise.

Serves 4 (three sliders per guest)

Ingredients

- One dozen slider rolls (such as King's Hawaiian®) or basic dinner rolls
- 1 lb. ground turkey
- 2 tablespoons soy sauce
- 2 fresh scallions, diced (optional)
- 8 slices of precooked bacon, cut into thirds (for a total of 24 pieces) and warmed
- 1 can chipotles in adobo sauce, 7 oz.
- 1 cup mayonnaise
- One or two ripe avocados, peeled and sliced

Directions

- Preheat oven to 350°. In a large bowl, combine ground turkey, soy sauce, and sliced scallions. Blend until all ingredients are thoroughly combined.
- Form 12 patties from the turkey mixture, each slightly larger in diameter than the rolls. Place, evenly spaced, on baking sheet (for easier clean-up, you can line the sheet with parchment paper.)
- Bake for 15 to 20 minutes, until turkey patties are cooked through—no longer pink in the middle and with an internal temperature of at least 165°.
- While the turkey patties are cooking, prepare your chipotle mayo. Put one cup of mayonnaise in a small mixing bowl. From the can of chipotles, add one or two tablespoons of the adobo sauce to the mayonnaise. Remove two of the chipotle peppers and finely dice. You'll have a lot of left over chipotles and adobo sauce, which you can freeze to use the next time you make this recipe! Add the diced chipotles to the mayo and adobo sauce, stir to mix well.
- Cut slider rolls in half. You know the rest: assemble 12 sliders with the turkey patties, 2 pieces of bacon, avocado slices, and chipotle mayo. Pairs excellently with hot French fries (you can serve extra chipotle mayo on the side for dipping) and a crispy dill pickle spear.

The Hopkinsville Goblins

In August of 1955, five adults and seven children—a group made up of itinerant carnival works and their offspring—were supposedly terrorized overnight in a rural Kentucky farmhouse by twelve to fifteen "goblin-like" aliens after a bright streak was seen to cross the sky and disappear beyond the tree line some distance from their location.

The party claimed that they had held off the attacking creatures for nearly four hours during the late-night to early-morning hours of August 21 and 22.

The aliens were reportedly between two and four feet high, with large, pointed ears, glowing yellow eyes, spindly legs, and claw-like hands.

When local authorities were informed of the encounter on the morning of the 22nd, a posse comprised of four municipal police officers, five state troopers, three deputy sheriffs, and four military police offices drove to the farmhouse to search for evidence. They found nothing of note other than signs of gunfire in the form of bullet holes in windows and screen doors.

Ufologist Jerome Clark, author of The UFO Encyclopedia: The Phenomenon From the Beginning, noted that none of the law enforcement officials found any evidence of a hoax. Another notable Ufologist, Allen Hendry, commented that the case was distinguished [from other alien encounters] by its duration and also by the number of witnesses involved."

If you're ever harassed by goblins (or aliens) in the middle of the night, put down your gun and invite them in for a snack instead. Try an offering of graham crackers with peanut butter and a glass of milk.

COOKING NOTES

FRESHWATER FIENDS

**BEAST OF BUSCO
CHAMP
LIZARDMAN OF SCAPE ORE SWAMP
HARRY THE EEL-PIG**

THE BEAST OF BUSCO

The legend of the Beast of Busco was born in the late 1890s, when a farmer named Oscar Fulk, living near Churubusco in northern Indiana, spotted a gigantic snapping turtle in a lake on his property. The creature was so large and so unnerving that he tried to warn others in the community about it, but nobody seemed particularly concerned and Farmer Fulk eventually gave up on his story.

Nearly fifty years later, the rumors took on new life when in 1948 two men who were fishing on the same lake also spotted a monstrous turtle. This time, people took the story more seriously. First regional, then national, and eventually even international news services began reporting on "The Beast of Busco."

It's not unimaginable to believe that a snapping turtle could reach such gigantic proportions. In 1999, alligator snapping turtle was shown at the Shedd Aquarium in Chicago, Illinois. The animal was believed to be sixteen years old and weighed 249 pounds.

Although alligator snapping turtles have an average natural lifespan of seventy years, scientists believe that under ideal circumstances they may live as long as two hundred years.

An ancient alligator snapping turtle, living unmolested in rural mid-west America, could easily reach a weight of 500 pounds or more.

The average alligator snapping turtle weighing around 20 pounds can bite with a force of 160 Newtons. They are lightning-fast and their jaws are very sharp. Imagine that bite multiplied by twenty-five and someone could easily lose an arm or a leg to the fearsome creature.

The legend of the Beast of Busco has been surprisingly enduring. A festival called Churubusco's Turtle Days is held annually in June, and features turtle races, a parade, and a carnival. If the Beast of Busco comes to your dinner party, he'd probably be happy with a few fish and snails, but you could make him really feel at home and honor him with the official dessert of Indiana: Sugar Cream Pie.

Common Snapper vs. Alligator Snapper: What's the Difference?

The common snapper can be identified by a smooth shell, oval head, and small beak. Common snappers usually weigh between 10 and 35 pounds. By comparison, an alligator snapper has a distinctly spiky shell, large head, pronounced beak, and can weigh in at over 100 pounds. Best practice is to keep your fingers (or other appendages) away from the mouths of both types.

SUGAR CREAM PIE

Sugar cream pie is exactly what it sounds like: a sweet, creamy filling baked in a flaky pastry crust. There's a bit of a debate about the inclusion of cinnamon when it comes to being an *authentic* Hoosier sugar cream pie, but the Busco Beast is unlikely to complain either way.

Serves 8

Ingredients

- 1 prepared pie crust (partially blind baked—see note below)
- ¾ cup white flour
- ½ cup dark brown sugar
- ½ cup light brown sugar
- ½ cup white sugar
- ½ teaspoon each cinnamon and nutmeg
- ¼ teaspoon salt
- 1 ½ cup heavy cream
- 1 ½ cup evaporated milk (not sweetened condensed milk)
- 2 teaspoons vanilla extract

Directions

- Preheat oven to 375°
- In a medium saucepan, combine flour, sugars, cinnamon, nutmeg, and salt.
- Add cream and milk, stir to blend ingredients.
- Begin cooking over low heat, stirring frequently.
- Once the sugars start to dissolve, stir constantly (still on low heat) until the mixture begins to thicken. Stir in vanilla extract.
- Pour into prepared, pre-baked pie crust and bake for approximately 40 minutes or until the filling is set. You may need to use a crust shield to prevent the edges of the crust from getting too brown.
- If you're feeling fancy, sprinkle the top with white sugar and cinnamon, then use a kitchen torch to caramelize into a sweet crispy topping, as on crème brulee.

Blind baking is a method of cooking the crust before the filling. Some recipes, like this one, call for partial baking, but some recipes will call for the crust to be completely baked. To blind bake a crust, place a piece of parchment paper inside the crust and fill it with pie weights to prevent the side from sagging while it bakes. If you don't have pie weights, you can use loose dry beans or rice*. Bake crust at 375° for 12 to 15 minutes or until light golden. Cool before use.

*If you do use dry beans or rice, save them aside in a zip-close storage bag or plastic container to use for this purpose again so they don't go to waste.

CHAMP

Indigenous Abenaki and Iroquois called the creature Gitaskog, but today the serpentine creature who inhabits Lake Champlain is affectionately known as Champ.

Champlain, which is bordered by Vermont and New York in the United States and Quebec, Canada, is the largest lake in the Adirondacks Region.

It's so deep that Benedict Arnold's ship, Spitfire, which was lost during the Battle of Valcour, lay undiscovered for over 200 years when it was finally found by a lake survey team in 1997.

If a 54-foot ship can remain hidden for so long, imagine what else could be lurking in the lake's murky depths!

The first recorded sighting of Champ by a European was in 1609, and there have been at least 300 sightings since then.

The famous Mansi photo, taken in 1977, is convincing evidence of the beast's existence. The photograph bears a striking resemblance to similar pictures of the Loch Ness Monster. Could they be long-lost cousins?

In his natural habitat, Champ probably feasts on fish and lake eel but over the years he may have acquired a taste for the local cuisine enjoyed by his human neighbors. How often has he caught a whiff of maple-cured bacon emanating from the galley of a Lake Champlain houseboat?

Champ would appreciate a serving of fluffy, buttery, melt-in-your-mouth pancakes dripping with pure, golden, Vermont maple syrup and a side of crispy smoked bacon. But if he's looking for something more like a midnight snack you could whip up the ultimate French-Canadian comfort food that is beloved on both sides of the Northern border: poutine.

PANCAKES WITH VERMONT MAPLE SYRUP AND BACON

Pancakes and bacon aren't just for breakfast! And let's be honest, pancakes are only a vehicle for the indescribably delicious Vermont maple syrup. Don't settle for substitutions. Real Vermont maple syrup can be a little pricey and difficult to find in some parts of the country, but it's worth the effort. You'll need an electric griddle, or a stove-top griddle or large skillet for the pancakes, and two baking sheets and parchment paper to cook the bacon.

Serves 4 to 6

Ingredients

- 2 cups all-purpose baking mix, such as Jiffy® or Bisquick®
- 2 medium eggs
- 1 cup milk or half-and-half
- 2 tablespoons vegetable oil (plus a little for greasing the griddle)
- 1 lb. maple sugar cured smoked bacon
- Vermont maple syrup

Directions for Pancakes

- Heat griddle or large skillet to medium, brush lightly with vegetable oil (or use cooking spray.)
- In a large bowl, mix eggs, milk, and vegetable oil.
- Add baking mix, breaking up any lumps, and blend thoroughly into the liquid mixture until smooth.
- Pour ¼ cupful (or slightly less) on hot griddle. When bubbles begin to form on the surface of each pancake, flip it quickly. Cook until golden brown on both sides.
- Serve, buttered, in stacks of three to four pancakes, top with Vermont maple syrup.

Directions for Bacon (Best Method)

- Preheat oven to 375°.
- Line two baking sheets with parchment paper.
- Spread the bacon strips out on the paper, about ¼" to ½" apart.
- Bake for 25 to 30 minutes, or until desired doneness. For extra crispy bacon, turn once during the baking time.
- Remove from baking sheets to a couple of paper towels to absorb remaining grease. Serve hot.

POUTINE

There are only three ingredients to poutine: crispy, hot French fries, cheese curds, and brown gravy. It's simply comforting and satisfying in all the right ways. You probably don't even need a recipe.

As with many regional dishes, poutine connoisseurs all have their preferences and passionate opinions about what makes the dish "authentic." Should the fries be straight or crinkle-cut, or hand-cut? The crinkle-cut variety is recommended here because all those little crinkles are so good at holding the gravy and melty cheese curds; but Champ probably won't care which type you use!

Serves 4

Ingredients

- Frozen crinkle-cut French fries*, such as Ore-Ida, 16 oz.
- Vegetable oil, for frying
- 2 cups Cheddar cheese curds
- 1 ½ cup Brown gravy—from a jar, a powdered mix (envelope,) or make your own from scratch!

Directions

- Cook French fries according to package directions.
- While you're making the fries, prepare the gravy. You'll want it really hot to semi-melt the cheese when you pour it on.
- Divide fries between four plates, top with ½ cup cheese curds per serving, then pour on the hot, brown gravy.
- Serve immediately: Don't burn your tongue, but poutine is best while as hot and fresh as possible!

LIZARD MAN OF SCAPE ORE SWAMP

The Lizard Man of Scape Ore Swamp is a menacing beast that lurks deep in the swamps of Lee County, South Carolina. The first report came in July of 1988, when 17-year-old Christopher Davis told local law enforcement that his car had been attacked by a creature that was around seven feet tall, three fingers, glowing red eyes, and skin like that of a lizard. The story ran in at least one hundred newspapers nationwide.

In August of the same year, an airman stationed at Shaw Air Force Base filed a report which stated that he not only encountered the Lizard Man but that he had also shot and wounded it. The police charged him with carrying a pistol, at which point he recanted his story and admitted that he made up the story to keep the legend going. This confession led to the additional misdemeanor charge of filing a false police report.

There were other similar attacks and sightings in the region over the next few years. In 2008, a couple in Bishopville reported damage to their car and although the nature of the attack is unclear, there were traces of blood on the car that turned out to belong to a canid species.

The nature of the Lizard Man of Scape Ore Swamp is unclear. He is aggressive and there is no indication that he has tried to communicate with humanity.

If he is the only one of his kind, it's possible that he is lonely and just needs a friend. Or maybe he's cranky because he hasn't had a good meal in a few years.

If you encounter the Lizard Man, try not to show your fear, and extend the hand of hospitality instead. Rabbits, mink, deer, ducks, crawdads, frogs, beavers, and myriad other inhabitants of the South Carolina swamplands undoubtedly feature prominently in the lizardman's diet. Take some cues from the swamp and offer your new acquaintance a bowl of crawdads (a.k.a. crayfish or crawfish) and grits. If your local grocer or fish market doesn't offer crawdads, you can substitute shrimp.

South Carolina's Other Lizard Problem

As if being home to a lizard man isn't enough, South Carolina has recently been plagued by an invasion of non-native tegu lizards. The beastly creatures are predatory omnivores, have a powerful bite, and can grow up to four feet long. Tegus are a serious threat to native species because they prey upon other animals and especially enjoy the eggs of ground-nesting birds such as quail and turkey. State biologist say that there have been 100 reported tegu sightings across 27 counties in the state since 2020 but so far only nine have been removed from the wild.

CRAWDADS AND GRITS

This recipe is a variation of traditional Charleston Shrimp and Grits. Unlike the original, however, it doesn't use a roux-based gravy. You can substitute shrimp if crawdads aren't available.

Serves 6 to 8

Ingredients

- 1 medium yellow onion, diced
- 3 stalks celery, diced
- 1 large green bell pepper, seeded and diced
- 2 tablespoons olive oil or butter, for sautéing vegetables
- 2 cups crawdad tail meat
- 1 lb. andouille sausage, diced
- 2 teaspoons Old Bay seasoning
- 1 can diced tomatoes, any variety, 14.5 oz.
- ½ cup vegetable broth
- Hot sauce such as Tabasco, to taste
- Hot grits, cooked according to package directions

Directions

- In a large skillet, sauté onion, celery, and pepper until tender and slightly browned.
- Add sausage. Cook on medium heat for approximately 10 minutes, stirring occasionally.
- Add crawdad meat, tomatoes, seasoning, and vegetable broth. Cook on low, stirring occasionally, until liquid is reduced by about ½.
- Serve over hot cooked grits with optional Tabasco sauce added to taste.

The Holy Trinity of Cajun Cooking

Green bell pepper, onion, and celery, know as the "Holy Trinity" of Cajun cooking, are key ingredients in traditional Charleston Shrimp & Grits, jambalaya, etouffee, gumbo, dirty rice, and many other yummy down-South meals.

The trinity can be added to virtually any soup, stew, chili, or stir-fry for added flavor and nutrition.

THE LOVELAND FROGMAN

The story of the Loveland Frogman began in Ohio in the 1950s when a salesman traveling a lonesome road late at night encountered three creatures standing beneath a bridge. He described them as being around four feet tall with leathery skin and frog-like faces. One of the entities was waving a "wand," which was giving off sparks.

Although the salesman probably just witnessed a couple of ugly kids sneaking a smoke, sightings and rumors of the Loveland Frogman continued throughout the years.

In the 1970s, a Loveland police officer spotted an unidentified animal that fit the description of the frogman, shot and killed it, and recovered the body.

There was no indication that the creature had been a threat to the officer or anyone else so, sadly, the poor animal—later determined to be a large iguana without a tail—was apparently killed *only* because it was unidentifiable.

If you ever see a creature that might be the Loveland Frogman, don't shoot first and ask questions later. Assume that he is friendly and ask him if he wants to join you for a healthful snack such as a fresh fruit salad of cubed pineapple, kiwi, blueberries, and strawberries drizzled with a little wildflower honey.

HARRY THE EEL-PIG

Kentucky's Lake Herrington is a manmade body of water that was created in 1925 by the building of the Dix Dam. The dam was a great engineering achievement at the time, covering over 2000 acres and nearly 250 feet deep—the deepest lake in the state.

But that's not the only notable characteristic of Lake Herrington. Almost as soon as the lake was created, people began to report sightings of a strange creature in the water. Quickly dubbed "Harry," the Lake Herrington cryptid is between eight and fifteen feet long, with an speckled eel-like body and the face of a pig.

It may seem unlikely that an unidentified and possibly prehistoric creature would inhabit a man-made lake, but it isn't implausible that the water from the dam could have opened a passage (or multiple passages) to a series of underground limestone caves. The Kentucky Speleological Survey has already documented five thousand caves in the state and believes there are many more yet to be discovered. Several of the known caves contain water, and not all have of them been fully explored, so it's very plausible that unknown, ancient species could still be lurking in the passages and subterranean rivers and lakes.

Andrias matthewi, also known as Matthew's Giant Salamander, is an extinct salamander that was native to North America. It is believed to be the largest salamander species to have ever existed and was approximately seven feet in length. While Harry the Eel-Pig doesn't necessarily fit the description of a salamander, he is around the same size and could easily be an evolutionary cousin.

Skeptics, and even cryptid researchers, largely ignored the eel-pig lore until 1972 when Harry was spotted by Lawrence S. Thompson, a professor from the University of Kentucky. Apparently, his position in the realm of academia gave him a little more clout than that of the average, everyday eel-pig spotter.

He saw Harry several times but was unable to identify him as any known creature. He was absolutely sure that Harry was an unknown species of animal. When asked if he be believed he had seen a monster, his reply was, "It's only a monster in the sense that one would call an alligator a monster if they had never seen one before."

So, what might Harry like to eat? There's not much evidence to go on, but he is apparently getting plenty of grub in Lake Herrington which is full of bluegill, catfish, several types of bass, and many other species of fish. Eels eat fish (and sometimes other eels) as well as insect larvae, worms, amphibians, roe, and water snails. Pigs, on the other hand… well, they'll eat almost anything.

If Harry the Eel-Pig joins your dinner party, fry up a plateful of fish and hushpuppies along with a side of collard greens.

FRIED FISH AND HUSHPUPPIES

Harry the Eel-Pig probably eats catfish, but unless you can get *really* fresh catfish you might want to stick with a mild white fish such as cod or haddock. Frying fish is just like frying anything else—it might take a few tries to get it right. Hushpuppies are essentially balls of fried cornbread. Hushpuppies should be crispy, golden brown on the outside and fluffy on the inside. For a complete meal, serve fried fish and hushpuppies with a side of Southern-style collard greens or coleslaw.

Ingredients for Fried Fish

- Vegetable oil, for frying (you can use the same hot oil for both the fish and hushpuppies)
- 1 lb. fresh catfish, cod, or haddock, cut into chunks or cubes about 2"
- 1 cup flour
- 1 cup cornmeal
- 1 teaspoon each Old Bay Seasoning, paprika, tarragon, and cayanne pepper
- 2 eggs

Directions

- Crack eggs into a bowl and beat until thoroughly homogenized.
- In another bowl, blend flour, cornmeal, and seasonings.
- Dip fish pieces into eggs, then into the flour mixture to coat. Set aside on clean cutting board or plate to let the fish "rest" in the coating, which helps it stick to the fish during the frying process.
- Fill a small saucepan 2 to 4 inches deep and heat to approximately 375°.
- Working in small batches (three to four pieces at a time,) fry fish until golden brown on the outside and cooked through. The fish inside should be white, opaque, and flake easily.
- Use a slotted spoon to lift from oil and move to a plate or baking sheet lined with paper towels to absorb extra grease.

Ingredients for Hushpuppies

- 1 box corn muffin mix, 8.5 oz., such as Jiffy®
- ¼ cup self-rising flour
- 1 egg
- 1/3 cup whole milk or evaporated milk
- ¼ cup grated onion (optional)
- Vegetable oil for frying

Directions

- In a bowl, combine corn muffin mix, flour, egg, milk, and (optional) onion to create a thick batter. It should be slightly thicker than regular cornbread or muffin batter.
- Fill a small saucepan 2 to 4 inches deep and heat to approximately 375°.
- Drop a rounded tablespoonful of batter into hot oil. If the oil is hot enough, the batter will float and lots of tiny bubbles will form around it. Only cook three or four at a time. Overcrowding the pan will cool down the oil and the hushpuppies won't cook as quickly, which will make them heavy and greasy.
- Fry until golden brown on the outside and use a slotted spoon to remove them to a plate lined with paper towels to absorb any extra oil.

TIPS FOR KITCHEN BUDGETING

- Even if you have an unlimited grocery budget, challenge yourself to plan for at least one SNAP-budget meal per week; it's a great exercise to help you focus on getting the most value and nutrition for your money. SNAP benefits for low-income families vary from by state, but as of the writing of this book SNAP allows around $2.83 per person, per meal. Your state SNAP website features recipes specifically formulated to accommodate a SNAP budget using nutritious, healthy ingredients.

- Buy and prepare food with an eye on future meals. For example, when whole chickens are on sale, buy two and roast them at the same time to save time and fuel. You can serve one chicken fresh and freeze the meat from the other to use in a meal the next week. A zip-close freezer bag of cooked chicken takes up much less space in your freezer than a whole chicken and will thaw more quickly as well.

- Visit yard sales, estate sales, or the homeware department of your local thrift store to look for quality used kitchen items such as cast-iron skillets, dutch ovens, casserole dishes, rice steamers, ladles, knives, etc. These items can all be sanitized and spiffed up with a little elbow grease if needed, and you can usually pick them up for less than half of the original price.

THE WEE FOLK

**GNOMES
BOGGARTS
DUENDES
MENEHUNE**

GNOMES

Unlike the cheeky ceramic statues that often decorate suburban gardens, gnomes are a diminutive, human-like race that traditionally live in forest and woodland habitats where they are thought to act as guardians of the plants or of nature in general.

Many other wee folk delight in bringing woe to humans through pranks and trickery, but gnomes are believed to be shy and peaceable. They would rather avoid humans than engage in such shenanigans. Perhaps they just have more serious endeavors to attend to.

The earliest stories of "gnomes" originate in Switzerland, but similar entities are known by other names throughout most of Europe. They are usually described as having large, dark eyes and the males seem to prefer growing out their beards. Gnomes tend to wear drab colors, perhaps to blend into their woodland surroundings.

The alchemist/physician/theologian Paracelsus drew his descriptions of gnomes from legends and tales that originally came from German miners. In these stories, gnomes were small human-like beings who lived underground and frequently tormented the miners who invaded their domain.

Although they are frequently depicted as wearing tall, conical, bright red hats, this seems unlikely. It would be difficult to maneuver beneath low branches and vines, though briars and brambles without a tall hat getting caught on something or knocked off, and the bright red would stand out from the surrounding environment—not the best choice of accessories for a species who want to remain hidden from humanity. Unless the red hats have a religious or cultural significance to the gnomes, they are probably a folkloric fabrication.

The gnomish diet consists of foods that they can easily forage in the forest. In Switzerland, this would include wild mushrooms, nuts, berries, ramps (a wild plant related to garlic and onions,) alpine lovage, apples, lentils, tarragon, rosemary, and even some grains.

If you are ever lucky enough to see a gnome, invite him or her over for dinner and cook up a big pot of vegetarian mushroom burgundy.

MUSHROOM BURGUNDY

A vegan version of the classic *beef bourguignon*, this is a rich, hearty stew that is traditionally served over hot mashed potatoes. The secret to this dish is "slow and low" cooking. You can make easy substitutions as suggested in the recipe to make use of what you have on hand—just like forest-dwelling gnomes would! You'll need a crockpot or slow cooker with timer settings.

Serves 6

Ingredients

- 3 cups coarsely chopped mushrooms such as white button, shitake, portobello, cremini, or a mixture of whatever is fresh and available
- 1 cup ramps, shallots, onion, or combination, diced
- 2 stalks celery, diced
- 2 cups vegetable broth
- 2 tablespoons tomato paste
- 1 cup burgundy (or any dry red wine)
- 1 lb. carrots, parsnips, turnips, or combination, diced
- 2 cloves garlic, minced
- 1 tablespoon paprika
- 2 teaspoons salt
- 1 teaspoon pepper
- 2 bay leaves
- 2 teaspoons dried basil
- 1 teaspoon dried tarragon

Directions

- Combine vegetable broth, tomato paste, and wine in the crockpot and whisk together until thoroughly combined.
- Add all other ingredients and cook on low for four to six hours, or until all vegetables are tender, stirring occasionally.
- Remove bay leaves before serving.
- Serve over hot mashed potatoes.

BOGGARTS

Stories of boggarts (or "bogeys") began in the Lancashire region of England in the same medieval period that brought us Arthurian legends and a proliferation of fairy tales. Unlike the more recent incarnation of boggarts as poltergeist-type ghosts, the bogeys of ancient fairy lore are flesh-and-blood beings that wreak havoc in the daily lives of humans.

Boggarts reportedly lurk about on lonely country lanes and fields, but they will sometimes take up residence in a house against the homeowner's will. The boggart is difficult to get rid of once he or she has moved in, especially in country manor homes and farms where they seem to be most comfortable. Being of a prankster or trickster nature, a house boggart will cause mischief such as causing milk to spoil prematurely, prevent bread from rising, breaking dishes, etc.

Boggarts do not like to be ignored and causing an offense to a boggart will often escalate his bad behavior. They like to receive gifts and tributes, but be careful what you offer.

In the tale of "The Barcroft Hall Boggart," the resident boggart was offered a pair of wooden clogs as a reward for being unusually helpful to the farmer by assisting in everyday tasks.

For some reason, the boggart was enraged by the gift of clogs and began a vindictive campaign against the farmer and his family.

If you ever find yourself cohabitating with a boggart, cook up a traditional Lancashire Hotpot and invite him to the table. He may reward you by *not* breaking your good plates!

The Boggart of Red Brook

In his book *Slaithwaite Notes; Past and Present* (1905,) author John Sugden shares the story of The Boggart of Red Brook.

According to Sugden, a frightful boggart patrolled the lonesome and rural road near Red Brook, threatening and terrorizing travelers into giving him money in exchange for safe passage.

The jig was up when one such traveler fought back, assaulting the boggart with a staff, only to discover that the phantom was just a man wearing a sheet. The false boggart begged for mercy, but the traveler tied him to the back of his wagon and immediately took him to the nearest public house where he was turned over to the authorities for punishment.

LANCASHIRE HOTPOT

As the name suggests, this dish originated in Lancashire, England. Although traditionally made of mutton—and some versions use lamb liver—today it's more commonly made with lamb or a tender cut of beef. You can use either or both!

This is a warm, comforting dish that not even the crankiest boggart could refuse. You'll want to cook this is a large dutch oven or a deep casserole dish.

Serves 4 to 6

Ingredients

- 1 ½ lb. lamb or beef stew meat, cut into bite-sized pieces
- ½ cup flour or cornstarch
- 4 tablespoons butter (divided)
- 1 lb. carrots, peeled and sliced
- 4 to 5 large potatoes —about 1 lb.—peeled and thinly sliced
- 1 large onion, peeled and diced
- 2 ½ cups vegetable, beef, or lamb broth (or, 1 ½ cup broth plus 1 cup of stout or beer)
- 4 tablespoons tomato paste
- 2 teaspoons Worcestershire sauce
- Salt and pepper, to taste

Directions

- Heat oven to 350°
- In a large bowl, combine flour or cornstarch, a pinch of salt and a pepper, toss in the meat and stir to coat.
- Melt 2 tablespoons of butter (or vegetable oil, if you prefer) in a large skillet or heavy saucepan. Working in small batches, brown the meat on all sides.
- Transfer meat to the dutch oven or casserole dish.
- Now gently fry the diced onion and carrots in the same pan, adding a little more butter or oil if needed. Cook until carrots just start to get tender.
- Add the onion and carrots to the meat in the casserole dish. Deglaze the pan with a bit of broth or beer to get every bit of flavor, then combine remaining broth (or broth and beer,) tomato paste, Worcestershire sauce, and a couple of tablespoons flour or cornstarch as a thickener. Stir to blend ingredients thoroughly, especially breaking up any lumps of dry flour, and simmer on low heat until slightly thickened to create a rich, flavorful gravy.
- Pour over meat and vegetables. Add additional salt and pepper at this point, if desired.
- Carefully layer potato slices across the stew, overlapping by about a third, until the entire dish is covered with potato slices. Melt the remaining butter and brush over the potatoes.
- Cover with the lid (or aluminum foil) and bake for about an hour, or until potatoes are tender. Remove lid or foil and continue baking for another five to ten minutes so the potatoes will get golden and a bit crispy.
- Serve hot.

DUENDES

Duendes are small, humanoid entities that are believed to be part of the goblin race. They are typically described as being about two feet tall and looking like "little old men" with long beards, although it's not clear whether this applies to both males and females of the species, or to males only.

Folk tales of duendes have been recorded for hundreds of years throughout Latin America. In fact, "duende" can be found in Spanish dictionaries dating back to the 1500s, where it is defined as a mischievous, goblin-like spirit, although the oral tradition likely dates back much further.

Like many of the fae folk, duendes love to play pranks on people—sometimes good-naturedly and sometimes malicious—but are responsive to receiving gifts and tokens. A mischievous duende can be "tamed" by offerings of trinkets, fruit, candy, coins, or even cigarettes!

The duendes like to cohabitate with humans and frequently live within the walls of homes, particularly in children's rooms. This may be that because duende, like pixies, have a child-like nature. In fact, their laughter is often mistaken for that of human children. It may come as no surprise that although somewhat naughty at times, duende are believed to be great defenders of their homes and of the human children who reside therein.

Duendes are known to be primarily nocturnal creatures who like to prowl about at night, somewhat like a night guard or watchman of the household… although they don't let this self-appointed vocation get in the way of having a good time. Many an insomniac has reported hearing duende laughter during the night as the little folk caper and dance about the household.

When living out in nature, the duende diet consists largely of fruit and foraged vegetables, but in towns and villages where they live in human households, they have become accustomed to eating and scavenging leftovers.

If you suspect you have a duende living in the walls of your home, show them that you appreciate their watchful guardianship of your home by cooking something special like delicious arepas. Crispy on the outside and fluffy on the inside, these cornmeal flatbreads are easy to prepare and can be served in a variety of ways.

BASIC AREPAS

Warm, tasty arepas are a great alternative to English muffins, bread, or tortillas. They are easy to make and can be piled with toppings like flatbread or split in half and filled like a sandwich. You'll need a griddle or large skillet (cast iron is preferable) if available.

Makes 8 to 10 arepas, depending on size

Ingredients

- 2 ½ cups warm water (or as needed)
- 1 teaspoon salt
- 2 cups finely ground masarepa (white cornmeal) such as Goya®
- Vegetable oil or butter, frying

Directions

- Combine masarepa and salt in a large bowl.
- Slowly add water until a soft dough is formed. Be careful not to add too much water.
- Cover bowl with a clean towel and allow dough to set for 5 to 10 minutes.
- Shape dough into patties, approximately 1/4" thick and around 3" in diameter.
- Heat griddle or skillet on medium. Brush lightly with oil or butter.
- Lightly fry patties until they are golden brown on each side and cooked through. They should be slightly puffy, crispy on the outside and fluffy and tender on the inside.

Top with your choice of proteins

- Shredded chicken (store-bought rotisserie is quick, easy, and flavorful)
- Shrimp
- Adobo chicken
- Ground beef or turkey, cooked with taco seasoning
- Refried beans
- Chorizo sausage

Add optional topping

- Salsa fresca
- Guacamole
- Shredded cheese
- Chopped/shredded lettuce
- Diced tomatoes
- Sliced black olives

MENEHUNE

The Menehune are a native race of small, stout, humanoid creatures who inhabit the forests and deepest valleys of the Hawaiian islands. These diminutive beings are known for being mischievous tricksters, master builders, and excellent craftsmen.

Hawaiian tradition says that these little people are between six inches to three feet tall, with stocky frames, round potbellies, and a fine covering of hair.

The lives of the Menehune are joyful and industrious. They are believed to live in small communities in the lush tropical forests where they celebrate special occasions with song and dance.

The Menehune love to engineer and build things. According to Hawaiian lore, the Alekoko Fish Pond on the island of Kauai, which is approximately 1000 years old, was built by the Menehune in a single day. The Menehune may have been the engineering masterminds behind many of Hawaii's ancient roads and buildings.

Although the Menehune live in secret, they would probably love to join your dinner party—especially if they are enticed by the sound of lively music and the scent of delicious food.

It's hard to know to know what the Menehune might like to eat, but if they've been at all influenced by modern humanity, we can speculate on what they would enjoy.

Hawaiians are known for their love of SPAM®, a state-wide tradition that goes back to World War II. They have also embraced the Asian cuisine that was introduced to them by immigrants from Japan, Thailand, and Vietnam.

When a tribe of hungry Menehune show up for a meal, treat them to a tasty and filling meal of homemade SPAM® Fried Rice. If you really impress them with your culinary skills, they may even reward with a new fish pond!

SPAM FRIED RICE WITH EGGS

Don't be intimidated by the number of steps in this recipe! You'll need three or four small bowls for the prep, plus a wok (or large skillet) to bring it all together. It's tempting to throw it all in a pan or wok and cook it all at once, but the results really won't be the best.

Serves 6

Ingredients

- 4 cups cold, cooked white rice
- 1 pkg. fried rice seasoning (any brand)
- 1 tin of SPAM®, 12 oz., original or low-sodium, diced into ¼" cubes
- 1 ½ cup frozen mixed peas and diced carrots
- 1 small onion, diced
- 2 or 3 tablespoons sesame oil, or as needed soy sauce, to taste
- 8 medium eggs
    - 2 beaten (to add to fried rice –follow directions below)
    - 6 fried (to be served on top of fried rice)
- 4 scallions, finely sliced (optional)
- Siracha sauce (optional, to taste)

Directions

- Place carrots and peas in a bowl, break apart any that are frozen together. They will thaw slightly while you are dicing the onion and SPAM®.
- Crack 2 of the eggs into a bowl and whisk until thoroughly blended, set aside until ready to use.
- Swirl 1 tablespoon of sesame oil in a hot wok to coat. Add diced onion and lightly fry until soft, add peas and carrots. Stir occasionally, cook until tender. Remove vegetables from the wok with a slotted spoon. Stir-fry SPAM® until browned and crispy, stirring occasionally to prevent burning. Again using the slotted spoon remove the SPAM® from the wok and set aside.
- Now it's time to cook the beaten eggs. Your wok should be really hot, and eggs cook at a relatively low temperature, so reduce the heat and pour the beaten eggs into the wok. Don't stir the eggs, just let them gently cook into a lovely yellow "pancake." When the edges start to look a little crispy, flip it over to cook the other side. This goes fast—it will only take a couple of minutes to the eggs to cook through. When thoroughly cooked, remove to a cutting board to cool. Cut into ¼" squares.
- Add a tad more sesame oil to your wok and let it get hot, over medium-high heat. Ensuring that all "clumps" of the cold rice are broken up, add about half of the rice to the wok and, working quickly, fry until most grains are golden brown. Remove from wok and repeat with the other half of the rice.
- Return all rice to the wok and add fried rice seasoning according to package directions. Stir until thoroughly blended, then add in the vegetables, SPAM®, and cooked eggs. Season with a few dashes of soy sauce, to taste.
- Cover the fried rice to keep it warm and prepare your eggs, either poached or fried.
- Divide fried rice evenly between 6 bowls or plate. Top each bowl with a fried egg. Sprinkle with sliced scallions, if desired. Serve with optional siracha sauce for those who like a little extra heat.

UNICORNS

Unicorns aren't quite "Wee Folk," but for many people they do inhabit the same magical, fantastical realm somewhere between our world and the supernatural.

Early Mesopotamian, Indian, and Chinese culture showed unicorns as being more goat-like in form and having a short, colored horn. The ancient Greeks did not think of unicorns as being mythological creatures but took their existence as a matter of fact.

Today's image of the unicorn arose around the same time of Arthurian legend, and conjures medieval themes such as fairy kingdoms, wizardry, enchantments, and knights on perilous quests. In these tales, the unicorn symbolized virginity, purity, and the triumph of good over evil.

A unicorn is approximately 90% horse and 10% magic. Horses like oats and apples. Enchant both the unicorn and human guests with the simple magic of scrumptious, warm, comforting apple crisp!

MAGICAL APPLE CRISP

You'll need 6 apples of any variety (cored, peeled, and sliced,) 2 tablespoons sugar, 2 teaspoon ground cinnamon (divided,) 1 cup brown sugar, 1 cup old fashioned oats, 1 cup all-purpose flour, and 1 stick (1/2 cup) cold butter.

Mix the apples, sugar, and 1 teaspoon of cinnamon in a 9" square baking dish. In a bowl, combine flour, oats, brown sugar and the remaining teaspoon of cinnamon.

Cut in the cold butter with a fork or pastry blender until it's "coarse crumb" texture. Sprinkle over top of apples. Bake in 350° for 35 to 40 minutes, until golden brown and bubbly around the edges.

Serve with a scoop of vanilla ice cream.

OTHER THINGS THAT GO BUMP IN THE NIGHT

**WAMPUS CAT
CHUPACABRA
MOTHMAN
SNALLYGASTER**

WAMPUS CAT

The wampus cat—aka gallywampus, whistling wampus, or just wampus—skulks the swamps and forests of Appalachia and the Ozarks. The wampus is a nocturnal creature that can walk on its hind legs, is sometimes said to have six legs, and has been described variously as an ancient species of giant bobcat, a cross between a cat and a dog, a woman-cat hybrid, or a form of shapeshifter. The feline aspect seems to be the only point all eye-witnesses can agree on.

Much like the chupacabra, the wampus tends to prey upon chickens and other small animals, although some reports suggest the cryptid is strong and vicious enough to kill dogs, mules, and even mountain lions.

In 1890 around Lake Norman, North Carolina, a catlike critter rumored to be the wampus killed several chickens, goats, and even dogs; and in 1918 the people of Knoxville, Tennessee were so bothered by a wampus that on Thanksgiving morning approximately seventy-five men set out to hunt down the "devil in the shape of a tiger" but they failed to find their quarry.

Twenty-eight years later, The Greeneville Sun reported that there had been sightings and reports of a wampus prowling a ridge in the region of Gethsemane, Kentucky. The beast had reportedly eaten dogs, pigs, and other animals in the vicinity.

In the mountains of Tennessee and parts of Appalachian Pennsylvania, children are still reminded that the wampus likes to stalk kids (especially the naughty ones) who stay outside after dark.

There continue to be sporadic reports and rumors of sightings throughout the area.

Nobody would want to get on the bad side of a wampus cat, so if you suspect one is prowling around your property, why not show some hospitality and invite it in for a hot meal?

The Mysterious Ozarks

The Ozark mountain range spans Missouri, Arkansas, Oklahoma, and Kansas, and Illinois. The region is steeped in folklore, mythology, mystery, and plenty of cryptids.

In addition to the wampus cat, the Ozarks are home to other scientifically unidentified creatures such as the Ozark Howler, Momo the Monster, Ozark Booger Dog, The Blue Man, Gowrow, Gollywog, Chaw-Green, Jimplicute, Stone County Monster, and Whangdoodle (a.k.a. King Doodle.)

For an aspiring cryptozoologist, the dark, isolated Ozark mountains would be a perfect place to begin an investigation. If even half of the legends are true, you may find a monster lurking around every corner.

SAUSAGE GRAVY AND BISCUITS

Sausage gravy and biscuits is a beloved comfort food in the Ozarks and Appalachia, so Wampus would definitely appreciate a plate of fluffy country biscuits topped with rich, creamy sausage gravy. Great for breakfast, lunch, or dinner (and a good cure for a hangover, if someone is around to make it for you.)

Use a prepared baking mix such as Jiffy ® or Bisquick® to make 6 to 8 biscuits. Try to time the baking so they'll be ready around the same time as the gravy so you can serve it together with everything as hot and fresh as possible.

Ingredients

- Six to eight hot, fresh biscuits
- ¼ cup flour
- Bulk breakfast sausage, such as Jimmy Dean®
- 2 ½ cups milk

Directions

- To make the sausage gravy, start with one pound of good-quality raw bulk breakfast sausage, any variety. Cook over medium heat, cutting any larges chucks into small pieces as you stir occasionally, until thoroughly cooked.
- Drain off approximately ¾ of the grease but leave a little in the skillet. Spread out the sausage in the bottom of the pan. Sprinkle a little flour evenly over the sausage, around ¼ cup.
- Stir so there are no large clumps of flour and it's blended with the sausage grease. This is going to thicken the gravy.
- Add milk, and simmer on low heat, stirring occasionally, until gravy is thickened.
- Split biscuits and spoon a generous portion of sausage gravy over each half, add salt and pepper to taste.
- Serve hot and fresh.

CHUPACABRA

Stories of the chupacabra began popping up in Puerto Rico in the 1990s. This Johnny-come-lately cryptid quickly gained folkloric status as a vampiric creature that is primarily described as being dog-like in appearance but often with a spiky spine and a semi-reptilian aspect, which had led to speculation that it may be a hybridization of some sort; possibly a government experiment gone wrong or an alien invention.

Since chupacabras first appeared in the '90s, sightings have been reported widely throughout southern American states although at least one witness spotted it as far north as Maine. Apparently a critter without borders, by the early 2000s there were chupacabras seen in Russia, the Philippines, Chile, and Mexico.

Unlike other cryptids, carcasses suspected of being chupacabras pop up on a relatively regular basis. The remains of numerous dog-like animals fitting the description have been sent for testing and the results have been consistently mundane: a canid (usually coyote or wild/feral dog) who suffered from mange.

One necropsy, however, came back with the verdict that the beast had "mostly" coyote DNA. *Mostly?* The nature of the non-coyote DNA was not identified, which could lead a conspiracy theorist to suspect a cover-up. Could this particular carcass have been the one that proves the theory that chupacabra has an otherworldly origin?

The diet of the chupacabra varies by region. Although in Puerto Rice the beast seems to prey primarily on poultry, it's also been known to drink the blood of goats, sheep, and other livestock.

In March of 2005, a story from central Russia claimed that 32 turkeys were killed by a chupacabra in just one night. When a "hangry" chupacabra shows up at your door, sooth his temper with an easy but delicious feast of savory turkey and stuffing.

TURKEY ROLL-UPS

This is a cozy comfort food that's easy enough for any weeknight and perfect to throw together when there is unexpected company. To make it even better, it's virtually fool-proof.

Serve with mashed potatoes and a hot vegetable side dish—classic green bean casserole, cranberry sauce, and dinner rolls makes this a festive "mini-Thanksgiving" meal! You'll need a 9"x13" baking dish.

Serves 6

Ingredients

- 12 slices of deli turkey, any variety, cut on deli slicer at thickness of 4 or 5
- 1 box of instant stuffing mix, prepared to package directions*
- 2 12-oz. jars of turkey gravy

*To make the stuffing extra special, add freshly diced apple, chopped golden raisins, dried cranberries, or diced onion to the water while it's boiling, just before adding the dried bread cubes. You can also add flavor by using low-sodium vegetable broth in place of water.

Directions

- Preheat oven to 350°.
- Place two slices of turkey out on cutting board or kitchen work surface, overlapping slices by about half.
- Spoon approximately one-sixth of stuffing across the width of the slices.
- Roll slices of turkey up around the stuffing and place in baking dish.
- Repeat with remaining turkey and stuffing –you should end up with 6 roll-ups.
- Pour gravy over the roll-ups, gently tip baking dish from side to side to get the gravy down into the sides of the roll-ups.
- Cover with aluminum foil and bake for 15 to 20 minutes or until the gravy is bubbling at the edges and thoroughly heated. Serve warm.

MOTHMAN

The Mothman, made famous by John Keel's "The Mothman Prophecies," is a relatively recent but terrifying addition to American cryptid lore. The first reported Mothman sighting came from Point Pleasant, West Virginia, in November of 1966.

Over the next few days and weeks, there were more reports of the winged monster.

Some reports assert that between 1966 and 1967 over 100 people saw the Mothman, but there may have been many other sightings by people who were too frightened to speak up.

The legend and rumors grew exponentially. Within a year, the presence of Mothman was directly linked to the collapse of Silver Bridge, as if the entity was a harbinger of doom. Not only that, but seemingly unrelated paranormal phenomena seemingly follow in the wake of a Mothman's appearance, such as UFO sightings and even a visit from the mysterious characters known as Men in Black.S

Mothman has not only been seen in Point Pleasant. A wave of sightings also began around 2011 in and around Chicago, Illinois. Many credible witnesses spotted a large, winged humanoid flying around the city and jumping from buildings.

Early descriptions of the creature say that he is a humanoid being approximately seven feet tall, a black body, white wings, and glowing red eyes. Is he more like a moth or more like a bird? It's hard to say, which makes theorizing about his food preferences a bit tricky.

Despite their reputation, moths do not eat wool or other natural fibers (it's the larvae or caterpillar of moths that are to blame.) Moths—like butterflies—ingest flower nectar, honeydew, and juices from decaying fruit. In other words, they like the sweet stuff. Moths, drink through a proboscis, but hopefully our Mothman has a human-like mouth.

When Mothman swoops in for your dinner party, start by offering him to a couple of sugary sweet treats like a Strawberry Float or a classic Ambrosia Salad.

Mind Your Proboscis

A proboscis is a tubular or straw-like mouth part found in many insects such as butterflies, moths, flies, and bees.

These insects use their proboscis to drink sap, nectar, fruit juice, water, or other liquids

STRAWBERRY FLOAT

This is a fun treat that nearly anyone with a sweet tooth will love! Use tall cups or glasses and be sure to provide drinking straws for guests who aren't equipped with a proboscis.

Serves 4

Ingredients

- Approximately 6 cups of Strawberry flavored soda, such as Fanta®
- Four large scoops of vanilla ice cream

Directions

- Pour soda into four tall glasses, about 1 ½ cup per glass
- Top with one large scoop of vanilla ice cream
- Serve immediately!

AMBROSIA SALAD

Six simple ingredients combine to make a classic, sweet, summery salad that has long been a staple of picnics and church potlucks. Mothman will love the fruity combination!

Serves 6 -8

Ingredients

- 1 cup mini marshmallows
- 1 cup pineapple chunks (drained)
- 1 cup mandarin oranges (drained)
- 1 cup sweetened, shredded coconut
- 1 cup maraschino cherries, drained and coarsely chopped
- 1 cup sour cream

Directions

- Combine the ingredients in a large salad bowl.
- Chill for 4 to 6 hours before serving.

SNALLYGASTER

The snallygaster is a cryptid with origins in Maryland but has also been seen in parts of Washington D.C. and West Virginia. The name is derived from the German term *Schneller Geist* or "quick ghost" and referred to an entity that was terrorizing German immigrants in the region of Frederick County in the early to mid-1700s. Although actual sightings were rare, the beast was described as a screeching dragon or bird-like reptile powerful enough to carry off men and livestock.

Rumors of the snallygaster persisted off and on throughout the region for around two hundred years but really gained ground in the early 1900s.

In 1909, a fearless group of men armed only with farming implements battled the beast for over an hour until it fled into the forest. *The Middletown Valley Register* ran a story about the encounter entitled "Scene and Incident of Snallygaster's Reign."

In 1934, the *Worcester Democrat* published an interesting account of a man named Mr. Lewis who killed a large, strange bird which was believed to be a juvenile snallygaster.

Like many cryptids, the snallygaster seems to have a fondness for raiding chicken coops.

If Snallygaster comes creeping around *your* coop, don't panic! Avoid a scene and incident by offering him a plate of Mamish Chicken and Gravy with homemade after-dinner Moravian mints.

PENNSYLVANIA DUTCH COUNTRY

With a moniker like "Pennsylvania Dutch," one might think that this community was founded by immigrants from Holland but in fact their heritage is primarily German. The "Dutch" part is an anglicized version of the German language, Deutsch.

The Pennsylvania Dutch community has their own language—what linguists have dubbed a "Rhine Franconian dialect"—that is a combination of both German and English.

Additionally, Pennsylvania Dutch isn't confined to the state of Pennsylvania. There are significant populations in New York, Ohio, Indiana, Maryland, Virginia, West Virginia, and North Carolina. There are an estimated 400,000 people living in American who identify as Pennsylvania Dutch.

MAMISH CHICKEN AND GRAVY

This is called Mamish Chicken & Gravy because it combines traditional Amish Pennsylvania Dutch Chicken and Gravy with Maryland Fried Chicken, which makes use of saltine crackers instead of the basic flour that is used in the Pennsylvania Dutch recipe. The chicken first gets fried, then baked in cream. As the chicken bakes, the cracker coating acts as a thickening agent to make a delicious gravy while the top of the chicken remains crispy-crunchy.

Ingredients

- 3 large chicken breasts, each cut into two or three cutlets
- 2 sleeves saltine crackers
- 2 eggs
- 1 teaspoon each onion powder, garlic powder, paprika, and black pepper
- Vegetable oil, for frying
- 1 ½ cup heavy cream or whipping cream
- 1 cup water

Directions

- Heat oven to 350°
- Crush saltine crackers into "fine crumb" texture. Two sleeves of cracks might be too much, but it's better to have more than you need. You don't want to have to stop in the middle of breading your cutlets to crush more crackers!
- Stir seasonings into the crumbs and place in a shallow dish (such as a pie plate.)
- Prepare a baking sheet, cutting board, or countertop with a piece of waxed paper or foil to put the chicken on after you've coated it in the crumbs. Allowing the chicken to "rest" for a few minutes helps the coating to stick to the chicken during the frying process.
- Beat the eggs in a large bowl.
- Dip each chicken cutlet into the egg, then roll in the crumb/seasoning mixture until thoroughly coated. Set aside on the waxed paper while you heat the oil or butter for frying.
- In a large, deep skillet, heat about an 1 ½ to 2 inches of oil until hot enough for frying
- Begin frying the chicken. Fry only one or two pieces at a time. This stage does not have to cook the chicken thoroughly because it will continue cooking when it's in the oven.
- Turn each piece once or twice to make sure it's golden-crispy all over. Remove to paper towels to absorb extra grease.
- When all pieces have been fried, arrange them in a single layer in a baking dish.
- Whisk cream and water together and pour over the chicken. The chicken should not be completely submerged; the tops should be at least ¼" inch above the liquid to make sure they stay crispy while baking.
- Bake for about an hour, or until the internal chicken temperature is at least 165°.
- For a traditional Pennsylvania Dutch meal, serve over hot mashed potatoes.

MORAVIAN MINTS

This recipe came from the Pennsylvania Dutch chapter from a very old book of regional foods of the United States. Sometimes called Dutch mints, these are easy (and cheap!) to make. Some newer versions call for using a double-boiler, but this isn't necessary and is not required in the original. You will need a candy thermometer for this recipe.

Ingredients

- 3 cups confectioner's sugar
- 1 cup boiling water
- 12 to 15 drops peppermint oil (to taste)
- 3 to 5 drops red or green food coloring (optional)

Directions

- Prepare a place for the candies to cool before you start cooking —line a couple of sheet pans, or a countertop, with waxed or parchment paper.
- Boil sugar and water to 238° or until soft ball stage.*
- Remove from heat and immediately add peppermint oil, beat until thickened.
- Drop a little less than one tablespoon of the mixture at a time onto your prepared paper to make approximately 50 candies.
- Allow to cool thoroughly before serving.
- Store in a cool, dry place (if the Snallygaster doesn't eat them all up in one sitting!)

*In the lingo of candy-making, soft ball stage means that a small amount of the syrup or mixture will form a soft, pliable ball when dropped into cold water.

THE ULTIMATE BEASTLY FEAST

SHRIMP COCKTAIL DIP

ROAST CHICKEN

SIMPLE MASHED POTATOES

ROAST PARSNIPS AND CARROTS

SUMMER CAKE

The Ultimate Beastly Feast

Now that you've made some new friends, why not get everyone together for a great, festive meal —no special occasion needed!

Don't worry about having fancy place settings or little details like matching silverware or water glasses. Entertaining doesn't have to be "big" or expensive.

Relax: Nothing needs to be perfect for your friends to have a perfectly good time.

This simple menu ensures that there's a little something for everyone, whether your guests are carnivores, vegetarians, or omnivores.

To get the party started, serve Shrimp Cocktail Dip and crackers/toasts with carrot and celery sticks or an assortment of olives.

In regard to beverages, you can ask your guests to "BYOB" or offer a couple of different cocktails or mocktails. It's also nice to have a pitcher of ice water available.

The main course of roast chicken, mashed potatoes, parsnips, and carrots is a well-rounded meal that is relatively simple and doesn't take a lot of expensive ingredients.

Conclude the meal with an awesome dessert.

Summer Cake is light, delicious, and practically foolproof. Despite it's name, this cake is good at any time of the year!

SHRIMP COCKTAIL DIP

This is an easy and delicious appetizer that can be served with crackers or on round toasts.

Ingredients

- 1 can cocktail shrimp, 6 oz., drained and rinsed
- 1 block of cream cheese, 8 oz., softened
- 8 oz. shredded provolone cheese or 5-cheese Italian blend
- 1 tablespoon lemon juice
- 1 tablespoon Worcestershire sauce
- 1 jar prepared cocktail sauce, 8 oz.

Directions

- Preheat oven to 350°.
- Blend cream cheese, shredded cheese, lemon juice, and Worcestershire sauce.
- Once thoroughly blended, gently fold in shrimp.
- Spread in small baking dish, deep enough to leave at least 1" between the cheese mixture and the top edge of the dish (so you have space to add the cocktail sauce.)
- Bake in hot oven for 20 to 25 minutes, or until hot and bubbly around the edges.
- Remove from oven and pour cocktail sauce over the top.
- Serve warm with crackers or toast rounds.

Get the Party Started!

Ice-breakers and party games get a bad rap but they really are a great way for guests who don't know each other to loosen up and share a little bit about themselves.

Classics like "Two Truths and a Lie" or "Would You Rather…?" are good conversation starters and can help guests get to know each other.

Help your guests focus on the things that they have in common. Stay away from potentially hot-button topics such as religion and politics.

Too often hosts and hostesses get so preoccupied with trying to make everything perfect that they end up missing their own party, so don't forget to let yourself relax and enjoy the companionship of your guests.

ROAST CHICKEN

Making a juicy, tender roast chicken is easier than you think! You need a roasting pan (or a baking dish) and a meat thermometer. You don't have to truss up the back legs but it does help the chicken keep it's shape while roasting. If you're making "The Ultimate Beastly Feast," plan on putting the parsnips and carrots into the hot oven after the chicken has been in for twenty minutes to half an hour so the chicken and vegetables will be done at the same time.

Serves 6 to 8

Ingredients

- 3 lb. chicken
- ¼ cup butter, melted, or olive oil (for basting)
- 1 teaspoon each onion power, garlic powder, tarragon, white pepper
- 1 lemon
- 3 to 5 stalks celery (optional)
- Kitchen twine (optional)

Directions

- Preheat over to 375°.
- Remove any giblets/gizzards/neck from the cavity of the chicken. What you to with them is up to you—you can stew/strain them to make a broth, cook them up to add to gravy, or simply dispose of them.
- Cut the lemon in half and put it in the cavity of the chicken to give it a little flavor boost. You can also add chopped onion, apple, or a combination of all of these things. You're not going to be eating any of it, but they all add moisture and flavor as the chicken cooks.
- Lay the celery, concave side down, on the bottom of roasting pan or baking dish. This creates a little trivet to keep the chicken up out of its own juices and fat while it cooks. This isn't strictly necessary.
- Tie the legs together to keep them from falling out to the sides during the roasting process. Again, this is not strictly necessary but it does make for a nicer presentation.
- Baste chicken all over with butter or oil, then sprinkle with seasonings.
- Roast on center rack in over for about an hour and fifteen to twenty minutes, or until thermometer inserted into thickest part reads at least 165°.
- Cut twine to release legs before carving into slices/pieces. Meat should readily come away from the bones and joints should twist apart easily.

SIMPLE MASHED POTATOES

Creamy mashed potatoes are a great side dish for nearly any meal. To determine how many potatoes you'll need, a general rule of thumb is about a potato and half for each person. If you are into meal planning, make twice what you'll need and freeze half in a zip-close freezer bag and include them in your menu for the next week. You'll need a large pot for boiling water.

Serves 8

Ingredients

- 12 potatoes (russet and Yukon Gold are recommended, but any variety will work)
- ½ stick butter (cut into cubes)
- 1 cup milk (more or less)
- Salt and pepper to taste

Directions

- Boil water in a large pot such as a stockpot or really big saucepan. Add a dash of salt when the water comes to a boil.
- Peel potatoes and roughly cut into eighths.
- Add (carefully!) to boiling water.
- Boil for 15 to 20 minutes, until potatoes are tender.
- Drain water, add butter begin mashing, adding milk gradually. Continue combining until desired consistency, adding more milk if needed.
- Serve hot with extra butter and gravy if desired, salt and pepper to taste.

Gravy—homemade or not?

There's nothing wrong with opening a jar of store-bought gravy or whipping it up from a powered mix. But if you're feelings adventurous, you can make your own gravy with "pan drippings" (the fat and liquid that come off the meat when it cooks,) corn starch, and a low-sodium vegetable broth.

A good ratio to start with is 2 tablespoons of drippings, 2 tablespoons of corn starch, and one cup of broth. In a saucepan, blend the corn starch and drippings, then stir until there are no lumps. Turn on low heat and gradually add broth, whisking continuously. The gravy should start to thicken. Continue cooking until thoroughly blended and gravy is desired consistency. Serve hot.

ROAST PARSNIPS AND CARROTS

Parsnips are an underrated powerhouse of flavor and nutrition. They basically look like a white carrot and have a similar but slightly stronger flavor. Parsnips are high in fiber and are a good source of Vitamin C, B6, magnesium, and iron. You'll need a large baking sheet, which you can cover with parchment paper to make clean-up easier.

Serves 8

Ingredients

- 1 lb each carrots and parsnips, peeled and cut roughly into fourths lengthwise
- 2 tablespoons balsamic vinegar
- A little less than 1/4 cup olive oil (just enough to coat the vegetables)
- Salt and pepper, to taste

Directions

- Preheat oven to 375°
- In a large bowl, whisk vinegar and olive oil.
- Add parsnips and carrots, toss to thoroughly coat.
- Spread out on prepared baking sheet, sprinkle lightly with salt and pepper.
- Roast for 45 to 50 minutes (should be tender enough to cut through with a fork.)
- Serve hot.

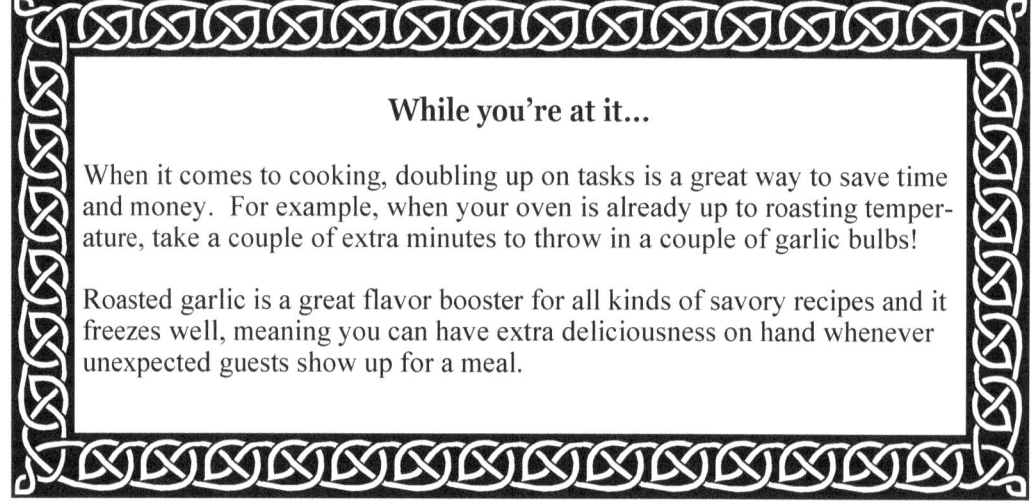

While you're at it...

When it comes to cooking, doubling up on tasks is a great way to save time and money. For example, when your oven is already up to roasting temperature, take a couple of extra minutes to throw in a couple of garlic bulbs!

Roasted garlic is a great flavor booster for all kinds of savory recipes and it freezes well, meaning you can have extra deliciousness on hand whenever unexpected guests show up for a meal.

SUMMER CAKE

This cake gets its name from the fresh, summery flavors of lemon and strawberry, but it's good any time of the year! Easy and full of flavor, this delicious cake makes a nice dessert for special occasions. The combination of lemon and strawberry is fresh and bright, and topping it with whipped cream instead of traditional frosting keeps it from being overly sweet.

Serves 8 to 10

Ingredients

- 1 box lemon cake mix—check package details for additional ingredients required such as water, vegetable oil, and eggs
- 1 jar strawberry jam, approximately 18 oz.
- 1 cup whipping cream
- 2 tablespoons confectioner's sugar
- 1 teaspoon vanilla extract

Directions

- Bake cake according to package directions for two 9" rounds and allow to cool completely
- Place one round of cake on a plate, spread top with a thick layer (approx. 1/8") of strawberry jam. You won't need the whole jar.
- Place the second cake round on top of the strawberry layer
- Pour whipping cream into a cold mixing bowl and begin mixing with an electric mixer. As the cream thickens, gradually add sugar, then vanilla. Continue mixing until the cream can form soft peaks or desired consistency.
- Spread whipped cream over the top of the cake. Cut into 8 to 10 slices and serve immediately.

SIGHTING/ENCOUNTER NOTES

ABOUT THE ARTIST:
ATLIT PRAMUDIO

Atlit Pramudio is an Indonesian artist with a passion for the field of art. He has loved drawing and creating unique works of art since childhood.

After completing his education, Atlit decided to share his knowledge and skills with the younger generation by becoming an art teacher, leading him to teach and guide students in developing their artistic skills for over twenty years. This experience not only enriched his own knowledge of art but also allowed him to develop effective teaching and communication skills.

He has recently decided to pursue his passion for art further by becoming a freelance illustrator, sculptor, and craftsman. He is particularly skilled at concept design and character development.

Atlit produces unique and interesting work for clients all over the world. He has a reputation for being amiable and easy to work with. He is successful as a freelance artist because he takes the time to listen to the client, understand what they are looking for, and engage them in the design process to make sure the finished product is exactly what they are expecting.

It has been a pleasure and a privilege for Strange Moon Press LLC to collaborate with Atlit on this project.

Atlit's portfolio can be viewed at www.fiverr.com/twintiger.

Strange Moon Press LLC
10 Benning St, Suite 160-168,
West Lebanon, NH 03784

strangemoonpress@gmail.com

www.strangemoonpress.com